Measure
for
Measure

by William Shakespeare

Anne Crow

Series Editors:
Nicola Onyett and Luke McBratney

Staffordshire

HODDER
EDUCATION
AN HACHETTE UK COMPANY

The publisher would like to thank the following for permission to reproduce copyright material:

Acknowledgments:

William Shakespeare: from *Measure for Measure* (1623); **pp. 1, 26: Daniel Massey:** from *Players of Shakespeare 2*, eds Russell Jackson and Robert Smallwood (CUP, 1989), by permission of Cambridge University Press; **pp. 10, 14, 38, 55: Carol Rutter (ed.):** from Clamourous Voices: Shakespeare's Women Today (The Women's Press, 1988), by permission; **pp. 24, 26, 29: Andrew Sanders:** from *The Short Oxford History of English Literature* (OUP, 1994), by permission of Oxford University Press; **pp. 36, 38, 41: Judith Cook (ed.):** from *Shakespeare's Players* (Harrap, 1983), by permission of the publisher; **p. 39: Michael Billington:** from www.theguardian.com/stage/2010/feb/19/ measure-for-measure-review (*The Guardian,* 2010), Copyright Guardian News & Media Ltd 2016; **p. 68:** from www.catholiccompany.com/getfed/virgin-martyrs-models-of-purity, copyright by The Catholic Company.

Photo credits:

p. 4: © Geraint Lewis; **p.12 (left):** © Geraint Lewis; **p.12 (right):** © JOHAN PERSSON/ArenaPAL/TopFoto; **p.28:** © JOHAN PERSSON/ArenaPAL/TopFoto; **p.34 (left):** © World History Archive / Alamy Stock Photo; **p.34 (right):** © Eliott Franks / ArenaPAL/TopFoto; **p. 53:** Tudor coin from the Asthall Hoard, 1470-1526 (gold), English School / © Ashmolean Museum, University of Oxford, UK / Bridgeman Images; **p. 54:** © Alx/Fotolia; **p. 60:** © ZUMA Press, Inc. / Alamy Stock Photo; **p. 61:** © The Granger Collection / TopFoto; **p. 62:** © REX Shutterstock

Although every effort has been made to ensure that website addresses are correct at time of going to press, Hodder Education cannot be held responsible for the content of any website mentioned. It is sometimes possible to find a relocated web page by typing in the address of the home page for a website in the URL window of your browser.

Orders: please contact Bookpoint Ltd, 130 Milton Park, Abingdon, Oxon OX14 4SB. Telephone: (44) 01235 827720. Fax: (44) 01235 400454. Lines are open 9.00–17.00, Monday to Saturday, with a 24-hour message answering service. Visit our website at www.hoddereducation.co.uk

© Anne Crow 2016

First published in 2016 by

Hodder Education

An Hachette UK Company,

Carmelite House, 50 Victoria Embankment

London EC4Y 0DZ

Impression number	5	4	3	2	1
Year	2020	2019	2018	2017	2016

Cover photo (and throughout) © Cristian Baitg/Getty

Illustrations by Integra Software Services Pvt. Ltd.

Typeset in Univers LT Std 47 Light Condensed 11/13 pt by Integra Software Services Pvt. Ltd., Pondicherry, India

Printed in Italy

A catalogue record for this title is available from the British Library

ISBN 9781471853890

Contents

Using this guide iv

Introduction vi

1 Synopsis 1

2 Scene summaries and commentaries 3

3 Themes 24

4 Characters 34

5 Writer's methods: Form, structure and language 44

6 Contexts 62

7 Working with the text 77

Assessment Objectives and skills 77

Building skills 1: Structuring your writing 82

Building skills 2: Analysing texts in detail 90

Extended commentaries 95

Top ten quotations 99

Taking it further 103

Why read this guide?

The purposes of this A-level Literature Guide are to enable you to organise your thoughts and responses to the text, deepen your understanding of key features and aspects and help you to address the particular requirements of examination questions and non-exam assessment (NEA) tasks in order to obtain the best possible grade. It will also prove useful to those of you writing an NEA piece on the text as it provides a number of summaries, lists, analyses and references to help with the content and construction of the assignment.

Note that teachers and examiners are seeking above all else evidence of an *informed personal response to the text*. A guide such as this can help you to understand the text, form your own opinions, and suggest areas to think about, but it cannot replace your own ideas and responses as an informed and autonomous reader.

Line references in this guide refer to the New Cambridge edition of the play.

How to make the most of this guide

You may find it useful to read sections of this guide when you need them, rather than reading it from start to finish. For example, you may find it helpful to read the 'Contexts' section before you start reading the text, or to read the 'Scene summaries and commentaries' section in conjunction with the text – whether to back up your first reading of it at school or college or to help you revise. The sections relating to the Assessment Objectives will be especially useful in the weeks leading up to the exam.

This guide is designed to help you to raise your achievement in your examination response to *Measure for Measure*. It is intended for you to use throughout your AS/A-level English Literature course. It will help you when you are studying the play for the first time and also during your revision.

The following features have been used throughout this guide to help you focus your understanding of the play:

Context

Context boxes give contextual information that relates directly to particular aspects of the text.

Build critical skills

Broaden your thinking about the text by answering the questions in the **Build critical skills** boxes. These help you to consider your own opinions in order to develop your skills of criticism and analysis.

Taking it further ▷▷

Taking it further boxes suggest and provide further background or illuminating parallels to the text.

CRITICAL VIEW

Critical view boxes highlight a particular Critical viewpoint that is relevant to an aspect of the main text. This allows you to develop the higher-level skills needed to come up with your own interpretation of a text.

TASK

Tasks are short and focused. They allow you to engage directly with a particular aspect of the text.

Top ten quotation

Top ten quotation

A cross-reference to Top ten quotations (see pp. 99–102 of this guide), where each quotation is accompanied by a commentary that shows why it is important.

Introduction

Measure for Measure is often called one of Shakespeare's 'problem plays' (see **Critical history**, p. 74) and not just because there are some inconsistencies, possibly created as the harassed playwright rushed the script to his impatient company of actors, or possibly mistakes made by Shakespeare's fellow actors who wrote the play down for the collected edition of his plays, published in 1623. It is difficult to classify a play which is at times hilariously funny and yet also potentially tragic. Shakespeare has fused elements of folk tales, the substitute bed-mate, the disguised ruler and the corrupt magistrate, with complex psychological analysis and weighty issues such as the nature of justice. These elements are not comfortable with each other and the result is that it is difficult to like or even admire the main characters, and the ending is not at all satisfying.

Measure for Measure can be performed as a conventional Renaissance comedy, entailing disguises, unlikely coincidences and an apparently happy ending, but this approach might fail to tackle the serious moral issues that Shakespeare raises. He seems to be challenging the glib expression 'measure for measure' and exploring themes suggested by this phrase, so that the apparently neat and harmonious ending is enigmatic and uncomfortable for the audience.

Different interpretations

It is important to remember that this is a script for a play which only comes alive in performance; it is not a novel, and it certainly was not intended as a text to be studied. *Measure for Measure* is a different play in each production, always fresh and interesting, because Shakespeare leaves so much up to the interpretation of the director and the actors. By contrast with the film of the Globe production in 2004, which concentrated on bringing out the comedy, the 1994 BBC production brings it dramatically up to date, making us aware that it deals with issues which still concern us today and really engaging our sympathies. Both of these productions are available on DVD.

But what is the playwright saying? Is measure really given for measure? Which characters does he want us to sympathise with? Are we supposed to approve of the outcome? You should have some lively discussions as you debate all the questions that are raised. Shakespeare provokes us to think about our attitudes to sexual behaviour, our understanding of justice, our expectations of a ruler; we have to face issues such as how to balance freedoms and restraint, justice and mercy, appearance and reality. The examiner will not expect you to have the answers, but will expect you to debate the issues intelligently, using the text to support your ideas.

Explore the craft of the playwright

Nevertheless, the play should not only be studied for its ideas, its plot and its characters. A-level students need to appreciate the craft of the playwright. Shakespeare's actors were all men and not very highly regarded in society, so you need to explore how his use of language helps them to sustain the illusion that they are dukes or illiterate fools, nuns or prostitutes. How does he manipulate our reactions to characters or events? How does he manage to make the audience feel important and involved in the story which unfolds before their eyes? How does he create ambiguity so that directors and actors can use their own personal responses to create a dynamic and challenging drama, still relevant today?

Shakespeare's *Measure for Measure* is set in Vienna at a time when the state is at war and there are hopes for a peaceful settlement. For at least 14 years, the Duke has failed to implement its laws, so the city is in a state of moral decay. Realising his fault but not wanting to suddenly appear tyrannical, Duke Vincentio plans to hand over his authority to Angelo, who has a reputation for virtue and moral strictness. The Duke plans to disguise himself as a friar in order to collect information about his subjects and keep a watchful eye on Angelo, whom he mistrusts.

Straightaway, Angelo decides that there is too much sexual licence in Vienna, and he resolves to strictly enforce a lapsed law. He orders the closure of brothels in the suburbs, and he wants to punish someone for unlawful sexual activity in order to deter other offenders. He cannot identify the father of a prostitute's child because they have several sexual partners, so his scapegoat has to be someone who is a faithful lover. Claudio and the woman he loves, Juliet, are engaged to be married, but, because her 'friends' refuse to release her dowry, they have not yet gone through the religious ceremony. It is therefore evident to all that the child Juliet carries is Claudio's. He is arrested for having sexual intercourse outside marriage and condemned to die.

Isabella, Claudio's sister, is about to enter a nunnery when her brother is arrested. She is virtuous and chaste, embracing the strict rules of the religious order and wishing they were even more rigorous. Claudio asks his friend, Lucio, to beg Isabella to intercede for him. When she reluctantly goes to Angelo to beg for mercy for Claudio, unaware that Claudio and Juliet are betrothed, he refuses, but suggests that there might be some way to change his mind, inviting her to return the following day. Angelo's asides make the audience aware that he desires the young virgin, but he has asked the Provost to remain during the interview so he cannot speak out. The next day, when they are alone, he offers to let Claudio live if Isabella agrees to have sexual intercourse with him. She is shocked and immediately refuses, threatening to expose him to the world as a hypocrite; however, she soon realises that no one would believe her. When she tells Claudio, he is outraged at first, but gradually his fear of death makes him try to persuade her to agree to Angelo's proposal. Isabella is horrified and turns against him, denouncing his cowardice.

CRITICAL VIEW

'God, in Shakespeare's time, was a living presence; you could be fined then for not going to church; suicide was the ultimate crime for the chilling reason that the culprit could no longer repent. In such an atmosphere, a dilemma such as Isabella faces about whether to sleep with Angelo, condemn herself to eternal damnation but save her brother's life, is seething with painful irony and hair-raising moral danger.'

(Daniel Massey, *Players of Shakespeare 2*, 1988)

Does this view help the audience to sympathise with Isabella's dilemma?

Meanwhile, the Duke, dressed as a friar, has been in hiding, listening to their conversation. He tells Claudio that he knows Angelo was merely testing Isabella, and warns him to prepare for death. He tells Isabella that Angelo's former fiancée, Mariana, was rejected when she lost her dowry in the shipwreck in which her brother died. The Duke knows that Mariana still loves Angelo, and he forms a plan by which Isabella will agree to have sexual intercourse with Angelo, but then Mariana will go in her place. The next morning, Angelo will pardon Claudio and be forced to marry Mariana according to the law, as their union will have been consummated.

Everything goes according to plan, except that Angelo does not pardon Claudio, fearing revenge. He brings forward the hour of execution and demands to have Claudio's head brought to him. The Duke, still in disguise as a friar, persuades the reluctant Provost to send the head of a pirate who looks like Claudio and has conveniently died of a fever, claiming that it belongs to Claudio. Isabella is not told of this substitution and believes that her brother is dead. The so-called friar tells her to appeal to the Duke, who is due to arrive shortly, accusing Angelo and demanding justice.

The Duke returns in his usual clothes, saying that he will hear all grievances immediately, at a holy fountain outside the city. Isabella publicly denounces Angelo, but the Duke pretends not to believe her. Mariana, veiled, reveals her part in the story and claims that Angelo is now her husband. Angelo denies the claims, saying they are malicious slanders. The Duke pretends not to believe the women and leaves the stage telling Angelo to enquire further, thus giving him a last chance to tell the truth.

Both women tell of a mysterious Friar Lodowick, who knew of their intention to accuse Angelo, and he is sent for. The Duke returns in the friar's habit, telling that he has been observing the corruption which has gripped the city in the Duke's absence. The so-called friar exchanges words with Lucio, with whom he had an altercation earlier in the play. Lucio pulls off the friar's hood, thus revealing the Duke's identity to the assembled company.

Angelo confesses and, unyielding to the last, repents and begs to be put to death. The Duke orders him to marry Mariana and then condemns him to death. Mariana begs for Angelo's life and pleads with Isabella to kneel with her. Even though she believes that Claudio is dead, Isabella does so, and she even finds arguments to offer in Angelo's defence. The Duke drags out the deception and continues to manipulate everyone, but eventually Claudio is summoned, reunited with his sister and commanded to marry Juliet. Angelo and Barnadine, a notorious and drunken criminal, are pardoned. Lucio is ordered to marry the woman who bore his child. The Duke asks Isabella to marry him, but Shakespeare does not let her answer him, so the end of the play is left up to the discretion of each director.

Target your thinking

- What is your personal response to the position of women as shown in this play? (**AO1**)
- Why does Shakespeare not give the audience all the information they need at the beginning of the play? (**AO2**)
- What opportunities are there for different interpretations? (**AO5**)

Timeline

Early modern playwrights were more concerned with the dramatic significance of events than with creating a detailed time frame for them. In *Measure for Measure*, Shakespeare uses the passing of time to create tension in the main plot, but he does not use references to time consistently.

Act I, Scene i

This is a public scene in which the Duke appoints Angelo as his deputy in Vienna and gives Escalus an unspecified commission before leaving the city quickly.

Commentary The Duke's opening lines are awkwardly expressed, suggesting he is ill at ease, lacking confidence in his plan. However, the convoluted sentence structure allows Shakespeare to open the play with the concept of 'government', a major theme.

Shakespeare holds back the fact that Angelo broke off his engagement to Mariana, so the audience is left wondering about the Duke's motives and what he knows about 'the kind of character' in Angelo's life. The Duke instructs Escalus not to deviate from his commission, so it seems his course is carefully planned. The Duke's abilities as a ruler are suspect when he suggests that Escalus' knowledge of the science of government exceeds his own, and then says he intends to make Angelo his deputy. The Duke has a particular reason for appointing Angelo **'with special soul'**; his questions to Escalus and his warnings to Angelo hint that he is testing his newly appointed deputy.

> Top ten quotation

In this opening scene, the themes of law, power and justice have been established; the theme of secrecy and deception begins with the Duke's clandestine departure. Whatever the explanation is for his drastic action of handing over the reins of power to a young, relatively inexperienced man, the Duke must have come to some kind of crisis point which has galvanised him into the need for action.

Act I, Scene ii

The scene changes to Vienna's underworld. Angelo has decreed that all the brothels in the suburbs are to be pulled down, but those in the city will remain because 'a wise burgher put in for them', indicating that somebody may be corruptly accepting bribes. Angelo is starting his period in office strictly, enforcing neglected laws. Claudio has been arrested for making his fiancée, Juliet, pregnant; before his execution, he is publicly humiliated as an example to others. Claudio asks Lucio to appeal to his sister, Isabella, asking her to persuade Angelo to be merciful.

▲ *Measure for Measure* at the Globe, 2015; the Globe emphasised the humour

Commentary The first recorded performance of the play was in 1604, when King James was negotiating a peace with Spain, and, in the play, Vienna is apparently negotiating a peace with Hungary. The brothel seems to be a regular meeting house for gentlemen, including Claudio who arranged to meet Lucio here. Lucio and two gentlemen briefly discuss politics, assuming that the Duke is on a secret diplomatic mission.

Shakespeare then introduces word play involving puns on the symptoms of sexually transmitted infections. Just as these gentlemen are infected with an incurable disease, so the body politic is suffering from too much licence, and Angelo plans to cure this by drastic surgery, reviving an old Act in which the punishment for fornication is death.

The Act is designed to force people to get married. Through registers of births, deaths and marriages, the state can gather information about people and keep control. Because it is impossible to control sexual behaviour completely, there will always be an excuse for rigid surveillance and repression. It seems that marriage is primarily concerned with the transfer of property; the only difference the ceremony would make to Juliet and Claudio would be the payment of her dowry. In Act III we learn that Angelo broke off his engagement with Mariana because her dowry was lost at sea, so that seems to have been his only motive for marriage.

TASK

Explain how 'Groping for trouts in a peculiar river' is an appropriate euphemism for Lucio to use. Make a list of other euphemisms Shakespeare uses for sexual intercourse and consider how appropriate they are to the speaker.

Shakespeare shows that, Claudio, while he clearly resents his arrest, nevertheless declares that it is 'just', and the result of 'too much liberty', introducing another theme. He knew about the 'drowsy and neglected Act' and does not dispute his guilt. However, Claudio is made the scapegoat because he and Juliet are faithful lovers; there can be no doubt that the baby she carries is his. Although Shakespeare shows Angelo to be unreasonably harsh, a modern audience might criticise Claudio for letting financial incentives prevent his marriage to Juliet.

He also selfishly expects his sister to use 'prone and speechless dialect' to persuade Angelo to be merciful. He wants to exploit her sensuality and puts that first; he expects that it is with her body rather than arguments that this girl who has devoted her life to Christ will influence Angelo.

Isabella is to enter the cloister 'this day'; the birth of Juliet's baby is imminent; a warrant has been issued for Claudio's execution. Time is of the essence.

Act I, Scene iii

The Duke has not left Vienna, but remains, disguised as a friar, to observe Angelo. As well as wanting Angelo to clean up the city, he wants to know whether Angelo's character will remain upright and puritanical, or whether power will reveal him to be a 'seemer'. The Duke tells Friar Thomas he has appointed Angelo to impose law and order on the city in his name, because it would be hypocritical if he were to have allowed liberty only to later enforce restraint.

Commentary The actors walk on **'in media res'** – in the middle of a conversation. This draws us straight into the conversation, seizing our attention and creating a sense of immediacy. Friar Thomas thought the Duke must be asking for a 'secret harbour' because he is in love, but the Duke vehemently rejects this notion. He declares that he has a 'complete bosom' and so is emotionally self-sufficient; the audience is left wondering why he thinks this.

In his description of Vienna, the Duke offers graphic imagery of the loss of order and restraint. The people are out of control, like weeds spoiling the harmony of the garden. They need to be controlled like horses, but with laws and punishment instead of bits and curbs. Animal imagery continues in pictures of himself as a lazy lion 'that goes not out to prey'. He then likens his subjects to children who mock threats of punishment because they are never administered. Because he has been like an over-indulgent father, anarchy has taken over. Worried about his public image, he wants to put things right but without appearing tyrannical. The Duke commands Friar Thomas to 'instruct' him how to impersonate a 'true friar', but dismisses Friar Thomas' valid point that it is his responsibility to put things right.

The backdrop of the war explains the lax attitude to sex, and the likelihood of peace explains the need to regain control and re-establish order. Possibly the Duke has been commander-in-chief of the army and so more concerned with fighting the war than ruling at home. Now that peace is imminent, he seems

Build critical skills

Lucio and Claudio are friends; why do you think Shakespeare has given Claudio speeches in blank verse while Lucio speaks in prose? (See **Verse** and **Prose**, pp. 55–58.)

to be turning his attention to his dukedom. However, he wants to avoid being seen as the source of repression, so he has appointed deputies and disguised himself as a friar so that he can gather information about all his subjects, from the highest to the lowest in society. This may seem laudable, but the disguise will give him access to people's private thoughts which they think are protected by the confessional, and it will allow him to advise and covertly manipulate his subjects. In III.i.52, the disguised Duke even manages to persuade the Provost to conceal him so that he can hear Isabella and Claudio's private conversation.

Shakespeare demonstrates the need for a ruler to understand his subjects and the need for the people to monitor the power and responsibility invested in the ruler. What Duke Vincentio is proposing is the Jacobean equivalent of Orwell's Big Brother in *1984*, a world in which everyone was under surveillance by the state (see **Contexts: *The Prince*, by Niccolò Machiavelli**, p. 73).

The Duke's strange behaviour in the opening scene is explained. Shakespeare's rhyming couplet at the close makes his motive clear. However, earlier in the scene, he admits that he has been negligent as a ruler and has chosen Angelo both because he will re-activate laws which have lain dormant and because Angelo is not going to take the people's affection away from himself. Shakespeare withholds the information that the Duke knows and disapproves of Angelo's betrayal of Mariana, but we learn that he distrusts Angelo because he seems to be too 'precise', too strictly puritanical; he thinks that, rather than being cold and unfeeling, as Lucio thinks, Angelo is 'at a guard' and holding in his passions. He suspects Angelo of being a **'seemer'**, and Shakespeare gives this view added weight by putting it at the end of the scene. Shakespeare has alerted the audience to be on their guard; Angelo may not be the only character who is not what he seems. The Duke is behaving in a way that makes the audience suspect his motives.

> **Top ten quotation**

Act I, Scene iv

Isabella is about to take holy orders and questions Sister Francisca about the rules of the order of Saint Clare. When Lucio comes to tell her of her brother's arrest, she does not believe him at first, but eventually she agrees to intercede on her brother's behalf.

juxtaposition: placing side by side for (possibly ironic) contrast of interpretation.

Commentary The Duke's doubts about Angelo are **juxtaposed** with Isabella wanting more restrictions than those offered by one of the strictest orders. It is unclear why she seeks 'a more strict restraint'; possibly, like Angelo, she is 'at a guard', holding in her passions.

As Lucio tries to explain Claudio's fault, he uncharacteristically speaks in blank verse and his imagery is elaborate and convoluted, perhaps because he is being awkwardly respectful in the presence of a virtuous woman, or perhaps he is mocking the sentimental language of love. He is similarly evasive when he tells her that Claudio is under sentence of death. He seems to genuinely admire her, 'as a thing enskied and sainted'.

TASK

Act out this scene, firstly demonstrating how Shakespeare exploits the comedy of a notorious libertine visiting a nunnery, and then presenting Lucio as a young man who is doing his utmost to help a friend in need, embarrassed by finding himself speaking to a nun.

Shakespeare makes Lucio withhold the fact that Claudio and Juliet have exchanged vows and regard themselves as married. This means that, when Isabella pleads for Claudio's life, the scene will be imbued with dramatic tension because she believes him to be guilty of fornication, the sin which she abhors the most. The scenes between Angelo and Isabella will hinge upon the conflict between a rigid interpretation of the law and appeals for mercy and grace, instead of a mere legal quibble about what kind of contract they had entered into.

Shakespeare exploits Isabella's reluctance to defend fornication, but Lucio is a good friend to Claudio, giving Isabella confidence in her powers of persuasion and urging her to act fast. **Ironically**, when he tells her to use her 'power', he then elaborates by telling her to 'weep and kneel'. In the seventeenth century, women's power apparently lay in their submissiveness. By the time he leaves, she sounds confident of success.

We learn that the Duke is seen by some of his subjects as a 'seemer', whose 'givings-out were of an infinite distance/ From his true meant design.'

Act II, Scene i

Escalus pleads for mercy for Claudio, suggesting it is possible that Angelo might have committed a similar sin. Angelo replies that justice can only concern itself with what it knows. It is irrelevant that he might 'have had such faults', but, if he were to commit the same sin, he should be punished in the same way. The comedy of the rest of the scene is mostly generated by Elbow's lack of understanding and his confused speech.

Commentary Shakespeare gives Angelo the definite **modal auxiliary verb** 'must' to demonstrate his inflexibility. He arrogantly thinks of the people's contempt for the law as like the contempt of carrion crows for a 'scarecrow'. Shakespeare continues to explore the theme of how a good ruler should impose law and order. Angelo assumes that the purpose of the law is to instil 'terror', as the Duke had told Escalus in the opening scene, but the Duke suggested that it should be balanced with 'love'. The Duke used the word 'terror' again to Friar Thomas when he explained that he had only used the law to frighten, as fond fathers use a birch rod.

Significantly, Angelo does not deny the possibility that he could be tempted, suggesting that his blood is not 'snow-broth' (I.iv.58), as Lucio claimed, but

irony: a use of language in which the implied meaning is different to the surface meaning. Irony can create subtle humour and/or make the audience think and appeal to their intelligence.

Taking it further ▶

From the information given in Act I, what can you deduce about what happened before the play opened?

modal auxiliary verb: an auxiliary verb used to express modality, i.e. degrees of possibility or probability.

Taking it further ▶

Do you agree with Angelo's argument that, in all cases, even though members of a jury may be worse offenders than the defendant, the justice of the sentence is not invalidated?

that he is keeping his passions under control. In Angelo's answer to Escalus, Shakespeare foreshadows later events and makes Angelo condemn himself to death (29–31).

As is often the case in Renaissance plays, comic scenes explore the same themes considered in the main plot. The theme of how the law should be administered and justice done is reworked with comic characters. On the street, the law is failing to control vice in the city because the office of constable is supposed to be taken by all citizens in turn, but the intelligent men pay fools like Elbow to do their stint. Elbow is not corrupt, but those who employ him as their substitute are, so the city has become debauched because of a failure to monitor the forces of law and order.

When asked whether being a pimp is a lawful trade, Pompey makes the telling observation that the law could be changed to make it lawful; laws are man-made and therefore not necessarily based on justice. Like Claudio, who disclaimed responsibility for his sin by claiming it was natural, Pompey offers the same male excuse, claiming that, if sex outside marriage is not to be allowed in Vienna, the authorities will need to 'geld and splay all the youth of the city'. If the punishment is execution, the state will be forced to legalise fornication within ten years because there will not be many people left. Through Pompey, Shakespeare demonstrates it is not possible to change people's behaviour or their characters by imposing laws.

Escalus asks, 'Which is the wiser here, Justice or Iniquity?' He is jokingly referring to Elbow and Pompey, but this parody draws attention to the way Shakespeare has set the pragmatic, but sinful, Pompey in opposition to the precise Angelo. Pompey shows up the flaws in Angelo's administration of the law.

Whereas Angelo soon leaves, announcing his departure in formal iambic pentameters, Escalus understands the bawdy innuendo and joins in the fun, pretending to find Pompey's defence valid so that he can hear Elbow's muddled responses. Elbow uses a lot of **malapropisms**, and Pompey deliberately goads him, knowing he will not understand. Escalus is more dignified, but, like Pompey, he encourages Elbow to make a fool of himself and makes puns on drawing and hanging that Froth will not understand.

malapropism: a confused, comically inaccurate use of long, sophisticated words (from the French '*mal á propos*', meaning inappropriate).

Shakespeare demonstrates why the Duke appointed Angelo as his deputy; Escalus is good-natured, merciful, lenient, and so unsuitable for the Duke's purpose. Having enjoyed Pompey's wit, he gives him a strong warning and releases him. Pompey procures women for men to use sexually; he exploits women without any sign of conscience. Through the irony that he is released while Claudio is condemned, Shakespeare highlights the problem of balancing justice and mercy.

At the very end of the scene, Escalus speaks to a character with a symbolic name. Significantly, Justice has been silent throughout the scene and he now condemns Angelo as 'severe' but says nothing about the bawds and the pimps.

It is eleven o'clock, reminding the audience that Claudio is to be executed at nine the next morning.

Act II, Scene ii

The Provost vainly reminds Angelo that judges have repented of imposing a death sentence. Juliet is in labour; Angelo orders that she be 'disposed of' to somewhere more suitable than a prison. Isabella seeks an audience with Angelo. She does not condone Claudio's behaviour, but she argues strongly that Angelo can and should remit the sentence. Lucio encourages her from the sidelines. Angelo tells her to come back next day before noon; the Provost is listening and realises that Claudio has a day's reprieve. Left alone, Angelo is amazed and confused by his desire for Isabella.

Commentary Angelo appears impatient with the Provost, brusquely dictating what should be done with Juliet and even suggesting that the Provost resign, a threat which must be exceeding his temporary authority. When Isabella seeks audience, Angelo is reassured by hearing that she is 'a virtuous maid', but, as soon as she appears, he tells the Provost to stay, suggesting that, at first sight, he is made to doubt his ability to remain coldly efficient.

Lucio is watching Angelo's reactions to Isabella, and he advises her to 'touch him, there's the vein' (line 72).

CRITICAL VIEW

Brian Gibbons, in the *New Cambridge Shakespeare*, explores this phrase in this way:

> 'that's the way to have an effect on him … "Vein" signifies "style" of writing or speech, but taken with "touch" alludes to finding a vein when blood-letting and hence "move emotionally". A direct literal sense may also be suspected: Lucio sees how emotion makes the veins stand out in Angelo's skin, and tells Isabella to reach out and touch him, to excite his pulse further.'

On line 129, Lucio speaks 'aside', so Isabella cannot hear him, using an ambiguous verb 'coming' which could be interpreted as suggesting sexual desire. This suggestion is confirmed by Angelo's own aside (lines 146–7).

Isabella establishes that she does not condone Claudio's behaviour. She has been pushed into arguing against her own moral compass. Her reluctance to perform the task imposed on her is shown in the internal conflict of lines 30–4. Shakespeare gives her the similar absolutes 'most' and 'must' to emphasise her abhorrence for Claudio's crime. Angelo speaks abruptly, trying to hurry her up. At Angelo's response, she gives up and turns away. Lucio pushes her to go back and try again. Once she begins to argue **semantics**, she is on more secure ground and holds her own forcefully, making Angelo admit that he has a choice. He cannot blame the law; it is his decision. His answer is brief, leaving her to undermine his argument in the rest of the line.

Build critical skills

Re-read Escalus' final speech of the scene.

- Explain his ideas of mercy and his feelings about Claudio's plight.
- Comment on the use of rhyme.
- To what extent are Escalus' ideas of mercy consistent with his earlier treatment of Pompey?

Context

In medieval medicine, blood was the humour associated with desire. If Angelo has been repressing his desires, the hitherto repressed humour might rush through his body all the more powerfully now that his desires are awakened.

semantics: the meanings of words, here the difference between 'can' and 'will'.

Shakespeare lets Angelo and Isabella share lines as the argument swaps between the two speakers, emphasising the tensions between them. Isabella gradually becomes warmer, more passionate in this battle of the sexes; she could also be interpreted as being aware of Angelo in a sexual way. (For a close analysis of this encounter, see **Extended commentaries**, pp. 95–6 and for an analysis of Shakespeare's exploration of what makes a just ruler, see **Themes: Power and responsibility**, pp. 26–8.)

Eventually, Angelo admits, in an aside, that he is attracted to Isabella, and he turns to leave. Her anger softens, and she twice asks him to turn back, offering to bribe him. As a nun, she has no worldly goods, so he might think she means to offer him sex. Is this what puts the idea in his head? How naïve is she? Is she really unaware of how she is tempting him? Lucio is definitely aware, and he is encouraging her, acting like a bawd to save his friend's life. Ironically, Shakespeare gives Isabella two conventional phrases of leave-taking which Angelo interprets literally, doubting whether he can keep his honour in the face of the desire he feels, and realising he should save his honour from being corrupted by her virtue. (For an analysis of Angelo's soliloquy, see **Soliloquies**, p. 48.)

Act II, Scene iii

Disguised as a friar, the Duke visits the prison and tries to make Juliet repent. He tells her that Claudio must die the next day.

Commentary The Provost tells the disguised Duke that Juliet has sullied her reputation, whereas he thinks that Claudio is 'more fit to do another such offence/ Than die for this'. In this society, a woman must be pure, but it is not so important for a man. When the so-called friar tries to encourage Juliet to truly repent rather than merely repenting out of fear of punishment, she interrupts him defiantly. When she learns that Claudio is to die next day, she bemoans the fact that her pregnancy saves her from execution and condemns her to **'a dying horror'**.

Act II, Scene iv

Angelo is alone, still struggling with his feelings and unable to pray. Isabella enters and, when he says that Claudio cannot live, she turns to go. This time they are alone. Angelo wants to keep her there so he suggests Claudio might be able

Top ten quotation

to live awhile. He hints at the possibility of her being able to save her brother's life, offering hypothetical cases. However, she fails to understand, so he has to ask her directly to have sex with him in return for her brother's life. Isabella is disgusted and accuses him of hypocrisy, threatening to tell the world. He replies that no one will believe her and leaves. Alone, she realises he is right and goes to tell Claudio, hoping he will sacrifice himself willingly to save her honour.

Commentary (For an analysis of Angelo's soliloquy, see **Soliloquies**, pp. 48–9.) Angelo's confession in his soliloquy ensures that the audience appreciates the double meaning of Isabella's innocent greeting, 'I come to know your pleasure', especially when Angelo replies that he wishes she understood without him having to make his desire known. When he says her brother cannot live, the audience once again, as in Act II, Scene ii, line162, understands the irony of her reference to him as 'your honour'. Shakespeare has given her conventional phrases of respect which are loaded with meanings, hidden from her but not from Angelo or the audience.

Isabella gives up quickly, so, to prevent her leaving, Angelo uses the modal auxiliary verb 'may' to offer a vague hope. Believing her brother guilty, Isabella asks to know when he will be executed so she can ensure that Claudio's soul will be saved. Angelo's inner torment is revealed as he rails against 'these filthy vices' of which he is also guilty now. Angelo equates creating a new life outside wedlock with taking a life, a manifestly unjust comparison to a modern ear, but he is a Puritan (see **Contexts: Shakespeare's world**, p. 66) and his interpretation of the Old Testament is rigid.

Isabella agrees that this extreme view is valid according to the Bible, but refutes the idea that man's law should punish them equally. This encourages Angelo to ask whether she would commit a similar sin to save her brother's life. Indeed he argues that it would be charity to do so. Possibly, as Angelo suspects, Isabella understands him and is deliberately leading him on, but her shock and horror when he speaks out clearly suggests that she is 'ignorant' of his true meaning. He recognises that they are talking at cross purposes, and she does not understand the 'sense' or meaning of his words; however, 'sense' also means feelings, and she is too unworldly to recognise his desire. (For some analysis of this part, see **Analysing texts in detail**, pp. 92–3.)

Angelo grows impatient and declares that he will 'speak more gross', but he continues to present a hypothetical case concerning 'such a person', and to use euphemisms, 'the treasures of your body'. She picks up his imagery and argues that she would undergo torture and death before giving her body up to shame (see **Isabella**, pp. 36–8, and **Shakespeare's world: Why Vienna?**, p. 68).

Angelo employs emotional blackmail, asking whether, by refusing to save her brother, she is as cruel as the judgement that condemns him. Isabella, however, has no doubts: she has a romantic image of herself as one of the martyrs she has been taught about who were tortured because they refused to give up their

> **Context**
>
> 'A bastard shall not enter into the congregation of the LORD; even to his tenth generation shall he not enter into the congregation of the LORD.'
>
> (Deuteronomy 23:2)

Build critical skills

Comment closely on the language of Isabella's speech beginning at line 150 (with the exclamation 'Ha!'). For what reasons do you think her tone changes so dramatically at this point?

TASK

List the arguments Angelo uses in this scene to try to persuade Isabella to have sex with him.

TASK

List all the references you can find in Acts I and II that suggest that Angelo is repressing his feelings. (For an analysis of Isabella's soliloquy, see **Soliloquies**, pp. 49–50.)

virginity. She would prefer death to dishonour and assumes that Claudio would agree with her decision.

'We are all frail', Angelo's reply to her apology, contradicts his previous attitude. Shakespeare leaves it open to interpretation whether he is cynically trying to influence her by telling her it is normal to be morally weak and sexually wanton, or whether this is evidence that he is beginning to realise his own weakness. Isabella accepts that, if her brother has been the only one to give in to the temptation, he should die. Angelo puts the blame on the woman as well, shamelessly arguing that it is understandable for a woman to be sexually wanton. Isabella accepts that women are easily taken in by men, and Angelo takes her words to be an admission that she is ready to give in. He encourages her to accept her destiny and act like a woman.

Believing he has persuaded her, Angelo tells her he loves her and says that her brother will not die if she gives him love. Shakespeare employs a pun when Angelo uses 'conceive' to mean 'understand', but Isabella picks up the meaning of 'fall pregnant' to draw attention to the parallel and the contrast with Claudio and Juliet.

Isabella's response to Angelo's proposition is not one we might expect of a naïve and unworldly novice. She throws his 'honour' back in his face, and attempts to gain the upper hand by defiantly demanding he sign a pardon for her brother or she will expose him to the world.

▲ Richard Dormer is a violent Angelo and Andrea Riseborough loudly protests

▲ Although Cheek by Jowl's performance is a very different take on *Measure for Measure*, the portrayal of Angelo is extremely similar

Angelo is confident she will not be believed and utters his final argument: if she does not give herself to him, then, instead of a quick execution, her brother will be tortured before he dies. From being an extremely virtuous man, Angelo, having given in to his 'sharp appetite', seems to have suddenly become an extremely vicious one. He can be interpreted as a ruthless sexual predator, acting with malicious intent, or alternatively as a naïve and inexperienced man, struggling to deal with desires and feelings he does not fully understand himself. Having committed himself to a course of action which actually disgusts him, he falls back on the realisation that, in the scales of public opinion, his now false reputation will 'o'erweigh' her true one. He is, of course, right; he is a high-ranking man of impeccable reputation, whereas she is merely a woman (see **Shakespeare's world**, p. 65).

Act III, Scene i

The Duke, disguised as a friar, tries to prepare Claudio for death. Isabella tells Claudio of Angelo's proposal and is outraged when Claudio begs her to submit. The Duke has been eavesdropping and suggests a plot to substitute Mariana. Isabella agrees.

Commentary Instead of preparing Claudio for death, the Duke delivers a homily on the futility of life. Claudio humbly thanks him, and, in a balanced and **paradoxical** statement, 'To sue to live, I find I seek to die,/ And seeking death, find life', Claudio declares himself prepared to die. However, his stoicism is rapidly dispelled when he learns of Angelo's offer.

Shakespeare has built up the tension around this first meeting between brother and sister. Claudio told Lucio in Act I, Scene ii of his 'great hope' in her persuasiveness. In II.iv.89, she sent word to him of her 'certain success', and in her soliloquy she expressed confidence in his 'mind of honour' (for a close analysis of this section, see **Analysing texts in detail**, pp. 90–1).

Claudio seems to assume he will be damned, and he imagines death in 'horrible' concrete images. He concludes that, however dreadful life is, it is a 'paradise' by comparison to 'what we fear of death'. His emotional speech encourages the audience to sympathise with Claudio, and this serves to harden attitudes to Isabella. When he begs her to let him live, she reacts violently.

> ### Build critical skills
>
> Why do you think Isabella is so angry? What evidence can you find to support each of the following possibilities? Does her anger comes as a result of her:
> - fear for her own immortal soul
> - disgust at the idea of sex
> - fear that she might enjoy sexual intercourse?

Her reaction to his fear suggests she is not suited to life as a nun. She abuses him cruelly, accusing him of 'a kind of incest', and doubting that he is their father's son.

Taking it further ▶

Act III, Scene i opens *in media res* (see p.5); imagine what Claudio and the Duke were saying before they entered.

paradoxical: apparently contradictory

> **TASK**
> List the Duke's reasons why death is to be preferred over life.

> ### Build critical skills
>
> Can you find any evidence to suggest that Isabella is either afraid of Claudio's reaction or embarrassed at her decision?

CRITICAL VIEW

'Isabella has a great need to wipe him completely off the slate. I think the journey Isabella goes through in the second half of the scene is a total annihilation of all values. His speech about dying is so deeply irreligious. It appals her.'

(Paola Dionisotti, *Clamorous Voices*, 1988)

Does this interpretation help to explain Isabella's violent reaction?

Isabella refuses to listen to Claudio, and the last words she speaks to him in the play are to accuse him of being no better than a bawd, willing to profit from his sister's shame, and to hope he dies soon because mercy would give him more opportunities to indulge in shameful acts. (NB see **Extended commentaries**, p. 97 for an analysis of their dialogue.)

CRITICAL VIEW

'Her vilification of her brother … shows her as an hysteric, as a neurotic, and it shows her as a religious maniac.'

(Penelope Wilton, *Shakespeare on Stage*, edited by Julian Curry, 2010)

Do you find this interpretation more appropriate?

The audience might have forgotten that the Duke is eavesdropping, or the director might have secreted him where the audience can see him. It would have been charitable in him to intervene earlier, and it appears voyeuristic that he lets Isabella continue her rant. However, he must have been surprised at Angelo's treachery; he could not have expected this, so Shakespeare suggests that he needs time to react to this new development and to decide how to proceed. When he does speak it is in prose, and this signals the release of the horrifying emotional intensity of the scene between brother and sister, and a change in direction to improvising a plan of action.

This is a turning point; from being an observer, Shakespeare shows the Duke begin to take control of events. Isabella is sharp with him, suggesting that she might be ashamed that a holy friar overheard her lose her temper; 'I have no superfluous leisure', she declares, but then she backs down and agrees to listen. The Duke lies to Claudio, telling that he is Angelo's confessor and knows Angelo's offer was merely a test of Isabella's virtue.

The Duke first asks Isabella her intentions, then, having learned that she is adamant, takes control. He wants to set a trap for Angelo who, as matters stand, could claim that he was testing Isabella's virtue. The Duke claims that his motivation is 'the love I have in doing good', but Shakespeare has made the audience aware that he is testing Angelo. He unfolds his plan, reassuring Isabella that she will be acting 'most uprighteously'. He tells her of how Mariana has been wronged, accusing Angelo of 'pretending' to discover that she had acted dishonourably and of **'unjust unkindness'** in his dealings with Mariana. Once again Shakespeare raises the question whether it is responsible in a ruler to knowingly appoint a liar and a hypocrite as his deputy. It appears the Duke was not merely testing Angelo, as he suggested in Act I, Scene iii, but seeking an opportunity to unmask him and 'advantage' Mariana.

Isabella reacts with the absolute certainty of youth and of her religious training; Mariana would be better dead than living with this stain on her reputation. The Duke now outlines his plan, and Isabella seems 'content' to deceive Angelo and send another 'maid' to his bed in her stead. However, this seems a hazardous strategy, and one might expect Isabella to be reluctant to put another woman at risk. Presumably she is easily persuaded because the man who suggests the bed trick is in a friar's habit, but this is a critical moment for her as she agrees to compromise her principles.

Act III, Scene ii

Elbow has arrested Pompey. When Lucio and the Duke, dressed as a friar, are alone on stage, Lucio utters some of the malicious gossip which has been spread about the absent Duke. Unable to set the reports right without giving himself away, the Duke protests and reveals his outrage in a soliloquy. Lucio has informed against Mistress Overdone, presumably bargaining for Claudio's life, and she denounces Lucio as the father of Kate Keepdown's child; he had promised marriage and then reneged on his promise. The so-called Friar and Escalus discuss the Duke and Angelo's sentence on Claudio. The Duke tries to justify his deception and manipulation of the other characters in a soliloquy.

Commentary After the tensions of the previous scene, a comic interlude is necessary, but, once again, the subplot explores the same themes as the main plot. The juxtaposition of Elbow's disgust with buying and selling men and women echoes the plan to swap Mariana for Isabella in the previous scene, and this link is enhanced because the Duke remains on stage. Lucio's broken promise of marriage to Kate Keepdown echoes Angelo's betrayal of Mariana. The Duke's disgust at Pompey and his trade may suggest that he is feeling guilty for behaving like a bawd, arranging a sexual encounter to catch Angelo. He reverts to poetry, and this may suggest that he has forgotten his disguise and is speaking as himself, revealing his inner emotions; he is angry at the depths of depravity in his city and realises he is responsible. Unlike a friar, he interrupts Pompey, not listening to his defence, and orders Elbow to: 'Take him to prison, officer'.

Much of the humour derives from the **dramatic irony** that the audience knows the friar's true identity. Lucio digs himself deeper into a hole, and the Duke is forced to listen to Lucio's calumnies. This conversation highlights the danger of a ruler keeping himself aloof from his people, because people will speculate about your reasons; however, the audience is left wondering whether there is any truth in Lucio's accusations. Lucio not only talks about the Duke,

> Top ten quotation

Context

According to English Renaissance law, if Mariana and Angelo sleep together, they are consummating the marriage vows they made on their engagement and so will be legally married (see **Shakespeare's World, Marriage Law,** p. 69).

dramatic irony: when the audience is put in the privileged position of knowing something the character speaking does not.

15

but also Angelo, saying that he is a puppet or 'a motion generative'. This is perceptively close to the truth; Lucio means Angelo has no feelings, like an automaton, but we know the Duke is pulling Angelo's strings. Ironically, Lucio's approval of the Duke's attitude to sex, that he 'would have dark deeds darkly answered, he would never bring them to light', is one of the slanders which outrages the Duke. He is learning about the responsibilities of a ruler and that his power cannot protect him from censure.

Shakespeare juxtaposes a scene with the witty, irreverent Lucio, in which the Duke learns what his subjects think of him, with a scene with Escalus, his trusted adviser. Escalus knows the Duke well, so the latter has to pretend to be a foreigner. His speech to Escalus reveals that his undercover spying has opened his eyes and made him totally disillusioned. Hurt by Lucio's slanders, the so-called friar asks Escalus about the Duke. Escalus replies positively that the Duke strived to know himself. The Duke is now learning, however, that this introspection is not enough for a ruler; he must also know his people and make sure that they know him.

The Duke's final soliloquy, in short lines and rhyming couplets, stands out from the play like a Chorus. He reflects first on the qualities necessary in a ruler, then on Angelo's failings, and finally on his own plans to put things right. God's deputy on earth should not just be holy, but he should be a pattern of 'Grace to stand and virtue go'; he should stand firm on the side of honour and benevolence and act virtuously. He should judge others by the same standards he sets for himself, unlike Angelo, who would kill another for a sin he himself would commit. To rectify his own laxity in allowing vice to flourish, the Duke has commissioned Angelo, but, in doing that, Angelo's own vice of hypocrisy has come to a head. In conclusion, the Duke justifies his deception and his manipulation of the other characters as 'craft against vice'.

Act IV, Scene i

Mariana is listening to a song when the Duke arrives and she soon leaves the stage. Isabella arrives and tells him the arrangements. While Isabella persuades Mariana to comply with the plan, the Duke has another soliloquy in which he reveals how disturbed he is by Lucio's slanders. Mariana agrees to the bed trick.

Commentary A boy sings of unrequited love, as Mariana broods on her lost love. She and the Duke think that her marriage contract with Angelo is still valid because it needed both parties to cancel it and so she readily agrees to the deception, convinced that consummation will make the marriage legal (see **Shakespeare's world: Marriage law**, p. 69).

She says that the friar has 'often' given her advice and calmed her 'brawling discontent', which suggests that Shakespeare intends to infer that either the Duke has adopted this disguise before, or that it has been quite a long time since he appointed Angelo his deputy.

The Duke seems nervous, reluctant to tell Mariana his high-risk plan, and he passes the buck to Isabella. Isabella, by contrast, has embraced the plot, adding details. This is one of the times when Shakespeare makes Isabella react like the heroine of the folk tale he used as his source, but this reaction is inconsistent with the complex character he has developed. When she asks Mariana to say 'Remember now my brother' as she leaves, it seems she has no qualms about putting Mariana in this position. This lends weight to the interpretation that she is very young and easily influenced by a man in a friar's habit, making decisions on her religious teaching.

Mariana is a recluse, living in a 'moated grange'; Isabella retired from the world behind the walls of a nunnery, and here we learn that Angelo has 'a garden circummured with brick'. These locations symbolise self-imposed restraint in contrast to those who visit crowded brothels and ale-houses where liberty prevails. Shakespeare implies that a moderate course between the two extremes is healthier.

Taking it further ▶

Note other times in the play when there is a conflict between the elements of folk tale and a realistic interpretation.

Act IV, Scene ii

Pompey is appointed executioner's assistant. It is midnight; the Provost tells Claudio that he must be executed at 8 a.m. The Duke enters, surprised that Isabella is not there, and no reprieve has arrived for Claudio. A messenger arrives from Angelo instructing the Provost to execute Claudio by 4 a.m. and send Angelo his head. The Duke had not anticipated this and tells the Provost to execute Barnadine and send his head. The Provost refuses because he has taken an oath, but the so-called friar argues that his oath was to the Duke, not the deputy, and produces a letter from the Duke, saying he will return in two days.

Commentary It is ironic that in Vienna the instrument of justice will be the character in the play most deserving of a severe sentence.

Build critical skills

A woman's virginity is also called her 'maidenhead', so Pompey, unabashed by his imprisonment, continues to play wittily with words; see also his **syllogism** on the word 'mystery' (lines 27–31) and the double meaning of 'for your own turn' (line 45). Why do you think Shakespeare has made this amoral person quick-witted and cheerful?

Abhorson is proud of his trade and resents having a bawd as his assistant. Like Angelo, Abhorson passes judgement on others whose sins are no greater than his own, without considering his own faults.

Build critical skills

Abhorson is given a vile name – a blend of 'abhorrent' and 'whore's son', and this name can sound like 'abortion' in production. Consider why Shakespeare has given his character this name.

syllogism: a form of logical argument that derives a conclusion from two propositions sharing a common term. Pompey argues that painting is a mystery, or skilled trade; whores are members of his occupation and they paint their faces, so he claims that his occupation is also a skilled trade.

The Duke enters with a cheerful greeting, suggesting he thinks his plan is being fulfilled at this very moment. The audience knows that, while this scene is being acted out, Angelo is having sexual intercourse with Mariana, thinking her to be Isabella. In his guise as friar, the Duke defends Angelo to the Provost, although, because of the dramatic irony, the audience probably assumes that he is deliberately trying to make Angelo seem worse when he is exposed by emphasising his 'great justice' and 'holy abstinence'. While the Provost reads the message from Angelo, the Duke has an aside in rhyming couplets in which he appears convinced that Angelo will pardon an offence so like his own. He seems to be hoping here that this situation will mellow Angelo, whereas before he has wanted 'the corrupt deputy scaled' (III.i.238–9), so that he will receive 'measure for measure' when weighed against his judgement of Claudio.

The Duke was not prepared for Angelo's betrayal and has to think quickly. He registers no shock or even surprise, suggesting that his resolve to unmask Angelo has hardened and nothing will stand in his way. Barnadine is to be summarily executed, and the Duke convinces himself that Angelo will not see the difference between Claudio's and Barnadine's heads. No longer diffident and awkward in speech, he almost bullies the Provost, who is sympathetic to Claudio but wants to keep his oath. Shakespeare shows that the Duke is so outraged at Angelo's behaviour that he seems to have forgotten his disguise and pushes his plan forward, ordering the Provost around with dukely confidence.

He reveals that the absent Duke either released prisoners or executed them, suggesting that, until now, he has seen offenders as guilty or innocent, not allowing any shades of grey. Also he has been out of touch with his people, not realising that Barnadine has been in prison for nine years. The Provost admits that the latter has the freedom of the prison and would not escape if he could.

Throughout the scene Shakespeare includes references to the passing of time and the approach of morning, adding tension to the Duke's persuasion of the Provost.

Act IV, Scene iii

Pompey observes many of the brothel's clients are in the prison. Barnadine refuses to be executed, even when the so-called friar tries to persuade him. The Duke thinks it would be 'damnable' to execute him, unprepared for death as he is, but he needs a head to send to Angelo. Providentially, however, Ragozine has just died. While the Provost fetches the head, the Duke plans to write to Angelo telling him the Duke is returning publicly and will meet him outside the city. Isabella enters; the Duke tells her that Claudio has been executed and his head sent to Angelo. He promises her revenge next day when the Duke returns. Lucio enters, gives sympathy to Isabella and continues to slander the Duke.

Commentary Angelo is being thorough in his attempts to clear the city of vice; the prison is full of erstwhile customers of Mistress Overdone's establishment. Comedy is often based on topical jokes and Pompey's speech includes jokes about sex, syphilis, borrowing money, fashion, etc., which may be incomprehensible to a modern audience.

TASK

Make up some jokes for a modern stand-up comedian to deliver as he looks out over the audience and picks out customers of the brothel.

Barnadine fulfils several functions. Shakespeare reveals that the prisoners set the agenda as Barnadine declares that, if they wish to speak with him, they must come to his 'ward'. The Duke learns that, when a ruler is face to face with a condemned man, it is much more difficult to sentence him to instant death; it would not only damn the unprepared offender, but be **damnable** in the one who gave the order. However, he needs a head, so he resorts to begging Barnadine to allow himself to be executed.

Top ten quotation

The Duke is not so merciful to Isabella, however, brutally telling her that Claudio's 'head is off, and sent to Angelo'. Shakespeare demonstrates that the Duke wants her to be genuinely angry when she confronts Angelo next day, and he wants to get the credit when he tells her Claudio is alive and her despair turns to 'heavenly comforts'. He channels Isabella's anger into patience; in front of the Duke she shall have revenge to her heart's desire when she accuses Angelo 'home and home'. This manipulation of the situation so that Angelo's accuser will be fired by suppressed anger contradicts his declaration that he will proceed with Angelo 'By cold gradation and well-balanced form'. The plan is coming to a head, and the Duke takes the Provost into his confidence.

The Duke may also be testing Isabella; perhaps he has already decided to offer her marriage, and, when she accepts direction from a friar, she shows that she can control her emotions. He is certainly abusing his disguise, persuading people to do things on the strength of his 'holy order', and advocating revenge.

Isabella is a passionate woman, not really fitted to be a nun, unless she wants that rigid discipline to keep her passions in check. On hearing of Claudio's death, at first she does not believe her ears, then she declares, 'I will to him and pluck out his eyes!' However, she calms down, listens to a man she thinks is 'holy', and agrees to be directed by him.

Act IV, Scene iv

The Duke has sent Angelo and Escalus contradictory letters and confusing directions without explanation. Alone on stage, Angelo reveals how deeply disturbed he is by his actions. He has made one mistake, and his life is changed for ever.

Commentary The audience knows that the woman Angelo had intercourse with was one who loves him and believes herself married to him, and that Claudio has not, as he thinks, been executed. His extreme anguish here gives an actor the opportunity to engage the audience's sympathy. (For discussion of this soliloquy, see **Soliloquies**, pp. 48–9.)

Act IV, Scene v

This brief scene shows the Duke, in his own clothes, giving the final directions to bring his plan to fruition. Friar Peter is ordered to do only what he has been instructed. The Duke tells the friar to bring trumpeters to the city gate.

Commentary This second short scene continues to raise anticipation in the audience, especially as we are wondering what the Duke has planned that he is adamant that Friar Peter follow his instructions, even though he may 'blench' at them. Since we know the Duke does not welcome the people's 'loud applause and aves vehement', he clearly has an ulterior motive for ordering trumpets and collecting 'the generous and gravest citizens' to witness the hand-over of power. Angelo's unmasking will be very public. By including this scene, Shakespeare reminds the audience what the Duke looks like without his disguise.

Act IV, Scene vi

Isabella tells Mariana of her reluctance to lie about events, since the supposed friar has directed her to leave the true account to Mariana. Friar Lodowick has warned her that she should not think it strange if he speaks against her. Friar Peter enters to take the women to a good vantage point, as trumpets have sounded and all important citizens have gathered.

Commentary Isabella is no longer as rigid in her moral attitudes. She has allowed herself to act against her better judgement and be directed by a man whom she thinks a holy friar. Friar Lodowick told her (IV.iii.137) that he will not be at the ceremony, so why has he warned her that he may play devil's advocate? In the final scene, the Duke does not speak against her 'on the adverse side' when he is wearing the friar's habit. It seems, therefore, that he may be confusing his two roles and thinking that, as the Duke, he will draw Angelo on with lies.

Act V, Scene i

At the city gate, the Duke hyperbolically praises Angelo. Isabella kneels and passionately demands justice. Angelo tries to forestall her accusation by saying she is mad with grief. The Duke pretends not to believe her, but then appears to waver, observing that she argues logically. Isabella trusts the friar enough to lie as she accuses Angelo. As Isabella turns to leave because her plea is rejected, the Duke has to have her arrested to ensure her return.

Friar Peter strangely testifies against Isabella, praising Angelo as a 'worthy nobleman'. Mariana enters, veiled, and speaks enigmatically, claiming Angelo is her husband. Angelo suspects the women are being manipulated by someone more powerful. The Duke sends for Friar Lodowick and leaves the stage, putting Escalus in charge. Escalus believes Lucio; he recalls Isabella. When the Duke re-enters in disguise, he says the Duke is unjust for making the accused man the judge. Escalus is so angry at this that he threatens to torture him. The Duke observes he has seen appalling corruption in the state. Lucio accuses Friar Lodowick of spreading scandal about the Duke and pulls his hood off.

Exposed, Angelo begs for death; he is commanded to marry Mariana. The Duke keeps Isabella in ignorance of her brother's reprieve. He condemns Angelo to immediate death. Mariana pleads for Angelo's life and begs Isabella to join her. After a while, Isabella kneels and finds arguments in favour of Angelo, acknowledging that her brother's execution was just. The Duke sends for Barnadine. Angelo expresses regret for the sorrow he has caused and begs to be put to death.

The Duke pardons Barnadine. Claudio is pardoned and ordered to marry Juliet. Lucio is forgiven his slanders but ordered to be married to the mother of his child. The Duke asks for Isabella's hand in marriage twice, but she gives no answer.

Commentary The Duke has planned this scene down to the last detail, and, in striking contrast to all the private scenes, he has chosen to make the final scene public, ensuring that Angelo's hypocrisy will be revealed to the whole city. Only he and the audience understand fully what is being enacted, creating much dramatic irony, such as the double meaning of the Duke's promise to Angelo of 'more requital' as either reward or retribution, and, when he says 'your desert speaks loud', the ambiguity continues to raise anticipation.

> **TASK**
>
> In Act III, Scene i, lines 135–47, Isabella is genuinely angry with Claudio, and Shakespeare reveals this in her language choices and the ways in which he breaks up the verse rhythms. In this final scene, Isabella has been made to lie, and, although she is upset that Claudio is dead, she still believes his punishment was just. Is it possible to tell from analysing her speeches in this scene, that she is not truly angry? (NB for a close analysis of lines 20–59, see **Extended commentaries**, pp. 97–8.)

Build critical skills

In what ways is the character of Isabella developing?

Isabella is courageous, considering the friar is not there to support her and the Duke appears to disbelieve her. She is not as fluent as she has been when spontaneously angry, but, each time she pauses, the Duke provokes her to argue her case more strongly, until she seems exhausted. He then appears to waver on lines 59–63, giving Angelo an opportunity to admit his guilt or embroil himself deeper in his web of lies. Angelo remains silent, but Isabella frames another balanced statement which supports her claim to be sane; in a carefully constructed **chiasmic** request she urges the Duke to 'make the truth appear where it seems hid,/ And hide the false seems true.'

At this, the Duke gives her formal permission to speak and she begins her story. The Duke speaks sarcastically, pretending not to believe her, and praises Angelo, pointing out how illogical it is that Angelo should execute a man for a crime he himself has committed.

Isabella appeals to heaven to help her keep her temper and to reveal the truth at some point in the future. With a final-sounding rhyming couplet she turns to leave. In order to keep her available and to give Angelo a false impression of safety, the Duke adds insult to injury by ordering Isabella to be arrested. He asks who knew of her intention, and she names Friar Lodowick. Lucio relieves the tension by compounding his own misdemeanours. Friar Peter, following the Duke's instructions, increases Angelo's sense of security by accusing Isabella of lying. Isabella is silent, either because she knows she lied in accusing Angelo of having intercourse with her, or because she has given up trying. She is taken away and Shakespeare brings in Mariana, veiled.

chiasmus: a figure of speech by which the order of the terms in the first of two parallel clauses is reversed in the second, which mirrors the key words of the first: '... truth ... seems hid/ ... hide ... seems true'.

Mariana speaks enigmatically; lines 183–6 are carefully prepared to sound like a riddle. She wears a veil, not only because it is necessary for the plot, but also to symbolise a woman's subservience to a man. She may not remove her veil until her husband bids her. As the Duke states, if she is 'neither maid, widow, nor wife', she is 'nothing', or, as Lucio suggests, a prostitute. Using Lucio's jokes and double entendres, Shakespeare presents Mariana's interrogation comically, thus heightening the shock for Angelo when her identity is revealed.

Since trying to forestall Isabella's accusation by claiming she is mad, Angelo has said nothing, although there is an implied stage direction suggesting that he smiles when Friar Peter says he will make Isabella confess she lied. He now speaks to express his confusion at Mariana's words and tell her to reveal her face. He admits breaking off the engagement, partly for her dowry falling short but then he repeats the slander of her damaged reputation, suggesting he is embarrassed to admit he only wanted to marry her for money. He now feels confident enough to speak out, accusing the two women of being set on by someone more powerful and asking permission to explore this further. Presumably he hopes that this will give him an opportunity to prevent the truth from ever being believed. The Duke sends for Friar Lodowick and leaves the stage – to don his disguise– without giving an explanation for his departure.

Escalus reverts to prose for business as he questions Lucio about Friar Lodowick and seems to believe his lies, even though his speech is full of sexual innuendo. In spite of his name, Escalus is not giving balanced judgement; he seems to be totally biased towards Angelo, and then, when the so-called friar accuses the Duke of injustice, his outrage makes him order Friar Lodowick to be tortured.

Shakespeare uses Lucio a) to liven up the story the audience already knows, b) to reduce the tension through dramatic irony as the audience anticipates his downfall, and c) to give Isabella moral support. The Duke gets more annoyed with Lucio every time he interrupts the carefully orchestrated plan. Having slandered the Duke to Friar Lodowick, Lucio compounds his offence by slandering Friar Lodowick to the Duke.

tragedy: a Shakespearean tragedy deals with men in high positions, with a fatal or disastrous conclusion for both the guilty and the innocent. A tragedy is characterised by waste, loss and a fall from power.

The Duke only recognises Lucio by his voice, so he must be keeping his hood low. The Duke resists arrest and, when Lucio goes to assist the Provost, the hood comes off in the struggle and the Duke is revealed. This is arguably the climax of the whole play, and Shakespeare engineers it through clowning around. By interweaving moments of low comedy with the serious drama, Shakespeare manages to lessen the **tragic** impact, and revisits his themes in a different way. Angelo is finally compelled to admit his guilt and, absolute to the end, he 'entreats' immediate sentence and death.

The Duke continues to lie about Claudio, telling Isabella to be happy that her brother no longer lives in fear of death. He employs the definite modal auxiliary 'must' as he orders Isabella to pardon Angelo. He makes a formal speech of denunciation, condemning Angelo to death, saying that he will achieve 'measure for measure', by having Angelo executed. However, it seems he has no intention of executing Angelo. Mariana begs for Angelo's life and entreats Isabella to kneel with her. The Duke makes Isabella's test harder by saying that he feels vengeance is reasonable. He has first-hand knowledge of her implacability, her passion, her sense of justice, and it seems he wants to break her, to make her kneel and beg. It takes 13 lines for Isabella to decide to kneel and find arguments in defence of Angelo. Using the modifying adverb 'partly' she says she thinks Angelo was sincere until he saw her.

Isabella still does not know that Claudio and Juliet had sworn a 'true contract' to marry (I.ii.126), so she argues that her brother's execution was 'justice'. After 'For Angelo', Shakespeare leaves the rest of the line blank, suggesting that she pauses as it is difficult for her to make this defence; however, she admits that, although he intended to rape her, he didn't. In spite of all that she has suffered, including the death of the brother she abused so strongly at their last meeting, Isabella is still able to support Mariana and plead for Angelo. She never speaks again. When Claudio is revealed, the Duke pardons him and in the same sentence he asks Isabella to marry him, as if she should agree out of gratitude. She does not reply to his proposal, and she does not say anything to Claudio.

CRITICAL VIEW

The classical Greek philosopher, Aristotle, defines a tragic hero as 'a man not pre-eminently virtuous and just, whose misfortune, however, is brought upon him not by vice and depravity but by some error of judgement'.

Shakespeare has posed questions, but he offers no answers; he is not a philosopher but a playwright, seeking to challenge his audience to think for themselves. Will Isabella accept the Duke's offer of marriage? Do Isabella and Claudio have a silent reconciliation on stage or were there words spoken that cannot be forgiven? Is there any chance that Angelo and Mariana's marriage will be a happy one? Three, or possibly four, marriages have been arranged which usually suggests harmony; is Vienna going to be a more harmonious, less corrupt city in the future?

Build critical skills

In the final line, the Duke says that, back in the palace, he will reveal everything they should know. What do you think he plans to tell them? Do you think the audience knows the full story or is Shakespeare suggesting that the Duke has still not revealed everything?

Build critical skills

What potential is there for *Measure for Measure* to become a tragedy? How does Shakespeare save the play from being a tragedy?

Build critical skills

If Angelo were sentenced to death, as he entreats, do you think he would be seen as a tragic hero, whose potential is undermined by a tragic flaw?

Themes

Target your thinking

- What is your response to the way aspects of love are presented in this play? (**AO1**)
- In what ways has Shakespeare set up a debate into the responsibilities of a ruler? (**AO2**)
- How does Shakespeare suggest that appearances are not always what they seem to be and different interpretations are possible? (**AO5**)

Shakespeare's themes in this play all stem from his exploration of the proposition in the title; in our individual lives and in government, a balance needs to be found.

Power   Responsibility

Justice   Mercy

Appearance and reality

Measure for Measure: Balance and equivalence

LOVE:
Sexual desire   Conscience

Liberty   Restraint

CRITICAL VIEW

'As its title suggests, Measure for Measure *offers a series of juxtapositions rather than coalescences.*'

(Andrew Sanders, *A Short Oxford History of English Literature*, 1994)

Using examples from the play, explain what you think this means.

'Measure for measure'

'A great play doesn't answer questions, it asks them.'

(John Mortimer, *Shakespeare in Perspective*, Volume 1, 1996)

In what ways does *Measure for Measure* ask questions?

Mortimer's view (p.24) is most certainly true of *Measure for Measure*. The title of the play is suggested by the Sermon on the Mount as reported in the Gospels (see **Sources and influences**, pp. 71–3). This quotation introduces the overall theme of balance and equivalence. The speech from which the title is taken is a ritualistic speech in which the Duke declares that order is now restored in Vienna, justice will be done and Angelo will be executed because he is guilty of a violation 'of sacred chastity and of promise-breach' (V.i.398). The quotation comes after he has declared that 'The very mercy of the law cries out .../ An Angelo for Claudio, death for death' (V.i.400–402). However, the audience knows that Angelo did not violate the chastity of a nun and that Claudio is still alive; the Duke is play-acting and he seems to have no intention of having Angelo executed as he believes Mariana's love for Angelo is genuine. Shakespeare shows that what may seem on the surface to be a balanced response is not.

At the beginning of the play, the Duke tells Escalus the power he has given Angelo has only been **'lent'** not given, and Angelo is merely **'dressed'** in his love. Angelo has been instructed to balance 'terror' and 'love', and, in line 44, he is told to balance 'mortality' and 'mercy', another pair of opposites. However, Angelo only *seems* to have the power of life and death; the Duke will retain the power and watch from the shadows in a disguise which he has been **'lent'**, employing the power to listen to confession and give advice that he assumes with the habit in which he has been **'dressed'**. Shakespeare creates a parallel situation in which, like Angelo, the Duke is wearing borrowed robes and wielding power to which he is not entitled.

The Duke admits that, in the past, he has been too lenient, and when he supposedly leaves the city, the symbolic character of Justice admits that Angelo is too severe. The scales of Justice have swung from one extreme to the other. One of the questions Shakespeare poses is whether balance has been achieved by the end of the play, but he has offered no answer; he has left the decision up to the director and the actors.

In his exploration of balance, Shakespeare has created situations which appear to be parallel but are, in fact, different. As we have seen, Angelo is wielding power that he has been officially lent for a short time; the Duke borrows a friar's robes and wields the power given by the church, but he was not given this power officially or even willingly. Angelo and Claudio have both had sexual intercourse without an official marriage ceremony; Claudio was condemned to death for this,

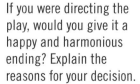

Top ten quotation

Taking it further ▶

If you were directing the play, would you give it a happy and harmonious ending? Explain the reasons for your decision.

so should Angelo be subject to the same punishment? Angelo and Claudio had both entered into pre-contractual agreements with their partners, but, whereas Claudio regards his as binding, Angelo rejected Mariana when her dowry was lost. Claudio and Lucio have both promised marriage and made their partners pregnant; in Act V, they are both told by the Duke that they must marry. However, whereas Claudio and Juliet love each other and they both want to get married, Lucio regards the marriage as a punishment and will no doubt prove a faithless husband.

CRITICAL VIEW

'Measure for Measure is a play of dark corners, hazy margins, and attempts at rigid definition. It poses the necessity of passing moral judgement while demonstrating that all judgement is relative.'

(Andrew Sanders, *A Short Oxford History of English Literature*, 1994)

To what extent do you agree with this reading of the play?

Balancing power and responsibility

CRITICAL VIEW

'Power, in all its manifestations, fascinated Shakespeare all his working life. Indeed, it preoccupied him with a creative intensity unmatched by any of his contemporaries. Not just the symbol of power, but, much more importantly, the human face behind it.'

(Daniel Massey, *Players of Shakespeare 2*, 1988)

The play was written at the beginning of the reign of King James I, and similarities between the king and Shakespeare's Duke are outlined in **Contexts**. Like James, the Duke believes that a ruler should set an example of virtue and restraint:

> He who the sword of heaven will bear
>
> Should be as holy, as severe:

(III.ii.223–4)

However, if a ruler lives like a monk, being 'holy' and 'severe', it will mean that he is not well known to his subjects and so all manner of rumours circulate, blackening his character. The Duke leaves quietly at the beginning, but he learns how some of his subjects interpret his actions and so, at the end, he returns with a triumphant ceremony. Part of the reason for this is undoubtedly to make Angelo's trial public, but the Duke has also learned to be more open with his people.

The Duke acknowledges that Friar Thomas is right to say that the responsibility to re-establish 'decorum' in the city belongs to him, but he dismisses the friar's admonition and uses his power to 'impose' (I.iii.41) this responsibility on another man so that he will not appear tyrannical. He then further abuses his power by making the friar give him a habit and teach him how to behave like a true friar in order that he might spy on his subjects, misleading them into thinking their confessions will be in confidence.

Gradually, the Duke learns that with power comes responsibility which he cannot escape. In the prison, the Duke learns that, although he has the power to order an execution, he also has the responsibility to ensure that the condemned man's guilt is 'most manifest' (IV.ii.122), and that he is prepared for death.

Angelo does not abuse his power in condemning Claudio, because even Claudio admits that he has broken the law. However, through Claudio, Shakespeare suggests mixed motives on Angelo's part; he is behaving tyrannically because cleaning up the city is his job, but he is also aware of his own 'eminence' (I.ii.145), a word that means both elevated rank and also personal ambition. Angelo is strict but he sincerely believes that he is prepared to accept the punishment if he were to commit the same crime; he declares:

> When I that censure him do so offend,
>
> Let mine own judgement pattern out my death,
>
> And nothing come in partial.

(II.i.29–31)

When he learns that he is not immune to sexual desire, his pride in his 'gravity', his honourable and dignified reputation (II.iv.9–10), makes him forget his 'grace' (IV.iv.31) and commit more offences to protect this reputation.

In the first scene between Angelo and Isabella, Shakespeare addresses the question of what makes a good ruler. Isabella agrees that Angelo cannot condemn the fault but not the perpetrator, but she argues that a ruler should exercise mercy, and reminds him of Christ's teaching. Through Isabella, Shakespeare succinctly sums up the need for balance in a ruler (see **Extended commentaries** for an analysis of their debate).

One of her most telling arguments is that someone with 'authority' should examine himself first; only through self-knowledge will a judge be justified in passing sentence on others. The irony is that Angelo is being beset by desire for her as she speaks, and when she leaves he asks 'what art thou, Angelo?' (II.ii.177), suddenly realising that he does not know himself. He realises that, just as a judge who steals cannot pass sentence on a robber, if he were to follow his new-found instincts, he will be unfit to pass judgement.

However, he fails to act on this self-knowledge; he blackmails Isabella and compounds the offence by hiding behind his reputation and threatening her that she will not be believed. As he says to her, using a metaphor of balance and equivalence, 'my false o'erweighs your true' (II.iv.171), meaning that his reputation will carry more weight than hers, even though he is false. He then abuses his power further when he breaks his word and orders Claudio's

Taking it further

Aspects of the play may have been inspired by Niccolò Machiavelli and *The Prince*, his influential treatise on statecraft, in which he argues that the effective use of power may necessitate unethical methods not in themselves desirable. Read the Contexts section on pp. 73–4, and then consider the extent to which you think Shakespeare intends the Duke to be played as a Machiavellian character.

Top ten quotation

Taking it further

For a detailed analysis of this speech, see *New Cambridge Shakespeare*, edited by Brian Gibbons, pages 33 and 177–8.

How far do you agree that 'The speech is a fierce effort to confront this guilt and confess it?'

Taking it further ▶

Listen to the *Arkangel* audio recording, which features Simon Russell Beale as Angelo. By the end of this soliloquy, the actor sounds as if he is nearly crying.

How far do you agree with this sympathetic interpretation of Angelo's realisation of the consequences of his loss of control?

Machiavellian: 'the employment of cunning and duplicity in statecraft or in general conduct' (*OED*). See **Sources and influences**, p. 73.

Taking it further ▶

In what ways could the Duke's behaviour be justified? Provide evidence from the text and, if possible, from productions, in your response.

Cheek by Jowl's production ▶ in 2015 focused on the corruption of the powerful

execution in order to cover up his sin. Shakespeare gives him a soliloquy in which he reveals his regret for, as he thinks, the violation of Isabella and the execution of her brother. His speech (IV.iv.18–32) indicates that he is ashamed of his behaviour, but he has too much pride in his reputation to admit his sins publicly.

When his guilt is revealed and he has no reputation to protect, he is at last able to reveal his 'penitent heart' (V.i.468). He has come to know himself and accepts responsibility for his abuses of power; he craves death, as being the appropriate punishment.

Shakespeare reinforces this essential attribute of a just ruler when Escalus tells the so-called friar that the Duke is 'One that, above all other strifes, contended especially to know himself' (III.ii.199–200). Although the Duke has shirked his responsibilities, he has apparently remained above the corruption in the state, but now, in his devious attempt to expose Angelo, he has abused his power in a **Machiavellian** way. He has spied on his subjects, made Isabella and the Provost act against their principles, lied to Claudio, abused the trust of Isabella and Mariana, cruelly lied to Isabella about her brother's death and then manipulated her to be grateful to him so that she will agree to marry him.

CRITICAL VIEW

Cheek by Jowl have produced a useful free education pack in which Peter Kirwan (of the University of Nottingham) says:

Where many of the city comedies of Shakespeare's contemporaries are now rarely performed under the assumption that they only address their own time, Measure for Measure's concern with social policy and urban governance continues to find more echoes around the world, making Shakespeare's view of the city one of his most enduringly contemporary achievements.

Search for news items that contain echoes of the play and consider when and where you might set a production of *Measure for Measure*.

Balancing justice and mercy

At the centre of Shakespeare's treatment of this theme is Angelo's judgement condemning Claudio to death for fornication. The so-called friar tells Escalus that Claudio 'willingly humbles himself to the determination of justice' (III.ii.209–10). Isabella, agreeing with Angelo's judgement, speaks of fornication as 'a vice that most I do abhor,/ And most desire should meet the blow of justice' (II.ii.30–1); however, she argues that 'neither heaven nor man grieve at the mercy' if Angelo were to pardon Claudio (II.ii.51). Here she separates divine justice and man's justice, but argues that both are improved when tempered with mercy.

CRITICAL VIEW

'Isabella's passionate and articulate defence of the concept of mercy in Act II is Shakespeare's most probing statement about the difficulty and consequences of judgement, but Isabella can be seen as arguing here as much from untried ideals as from an instinctive or acquired wisdom.'

(Andrew Sanders, *A Short Oxford History of English Literature*, 1994)

> **Taking it further** ▶▶
>
> In your own words, explain what Andrew Sanders means. How far do you agree with his assessment of Isabella and Shakespeare's presentation of her ideas?

Isabella lists the outward symbols of power wielded by men in authority, and she concludes that none of them **'Become them with one half so good a grace/ As mercy does'** (II.ii.63–4), ending on a half-line as if she is expecting Angelo to reply, but her argument has silenced him.

> Top ten quotation

Isabella's plea at the beginning of the final scene starts and finishes with a passionate demand for 'justice', by which she seems to mean that she wants Angelo to be judged according to the same standard of justice as Claudio. Persuaded to plead for Angelo, still thinking that Claudio has been beheaded, she admits, 'My brother had but justice,/ In that he did the thing for which he died' (V.i.441–2).

Angelo's guilt does not negate the justice of Claudio's sentence. As Angelo says before he meets Isabella, 'what's open made to justice,/ That justice seizes' (II.i.21–2). Justice can only concern itself with what it knows. At the end of that speech, he is confident enough in his own virtue to say: **'Let mine own judgement pattern out my death/ And nothing come in partial'** (II.i.30–1). When his attempts to hide behind his reputation have failed, and his guilt is exposed, he does not beg for mercy but makes the same argument that death is his 'deserving' (V.i.470).

> Top ten quotation

> ### Build critical skills
>
> In Act II, Scene i, Elbow has arrested Pompey and Froth. Compare Angelo's judgement on Froth with the way in which Escalus deals with this offender.

Escalus argues that all men are potentially guilty; even Angelo must have had the same thoughts as Claudio at some point, and so he should be merciful. However, he does not argue his case very strongly, merely observing that 'some rise by sin and some by virtue fall' (II.i.38). It is the Provost who is more concerned about Claudio; he argues that Angelo might regret his judgement too late, and he allows the so-called friar to persuade him to disobey Angelo's instructions. He even suggests the substitution of Ragozine's head. Whereas Escalus is a statesman, the Provost has responsibility for the care of prisoners, and so his sympathy for the prisoners supports the lesson the Duke learns that it is more difficult for a ruler to pronounce sentence of death when he is faced with the condemned man.

Taking it further ▶

At which points in the play could a production include gestures which might show the Duke falling in love with Isabella?

Quote and explain what gestures the actors could use. You may wish to refer to some productions in your response.

Love: balancing sexual desire with conscience

The Duke thinks at first that he will not be affected by 'the dribbling dart of love', assuming that Cupid's arrow will be too feeble to pierce his 'complete bosom' (I.iii.2–3). However, he gains more self-knowledge during the play. Shakespeare does not make it clear at what point he decides to ask Isabella to marry him, but productions sometimes use stage business to suggest this so that the ending does not come as a complete shock. Shakespeare does not reveal whether he has fallen in love with her, or whether, having tested her character *in extremis*, he thinks that with her chastity and her newly learned charity she will be a suitable spouse for a Duke. There is no indication that Isabella falls in love with him, however; indeed, in his disguise as a friar it would not occur to her.

Like the Duke, until Angelo met Isabella, he believed he was immune from the temptation of sexual desire, but he learns that 'Most dangerous/ Is that temptation that doth goad us on/ To sin in loving virtue.' (II.ii.185–7). He seems to think it is his love of Isabella's virtue that has overwhelmed him. Having repressed his natural instinct, when it is aroused he reacts violently, unable to achieve the balance expected in normal relationships. After a night struggling with his conscience and trying to pray but unable to stop thinking of Isabella, he decides to give his passion free rein: 'Blood, thou art blood' (II.iv.15). He is an absolutist, seemingly unable to compromise. As a Puritan (see **Contexts**, p. 66), he believes he has already sinned in desiring Isabella. Angelo's strict imposition of the laws is compared by Claudio with a new rider who uses spurs on the horse immediately he mounts in order to establish his control. This image could represent his sexual desires which are kept under strict restraint, but, when they are released, run rampant, like a wild horse released from the rein.

In Angelo's imagery, he equates Isabella with the nunnery: 'Having waste ground enough/ Shall we desire to raze the sanctuary/ And pitch our evils there?' (II.ii.174–6). It seems that part of the temptation for him is to destroy someone pure and untouchable; the devil has used another saintly person to trap him. As he says, he desires her 'foully for those things/ That make her good' (II.ii.178–9). His austere devotion to study and clean living has, through repression, been warped. He tells her that he loves her (II.iv.142), and in his next speech, 'He shall not, Isabel, if you give me love', makes it clear that to him love means sexual desire, and for him the two are mutually exclusive; if he were to follow his conscience he would say nothing to her.

Angelo's proposal of marriage to Mariana was not made out of love, as he broke off the engagement when her dowry was lost. Mariana's love for him, however,

> Top ten quotation

grew **'more violent and unruly'** as a result of his **'unjust unkindness'** (III.i.227–9). Suffering the pain of unrequited love, she has imposed isolation and restraint on herself in a 'moated grange' (III.i.247–8); this, however, has done little to still the 'brawling discontent' (IV.i.9) of her sexual desire, although the so-called friar manages to calm her.

By contrast, when Claudio speaks of love, he uses the plural determiner 'our', because theirs is a mutual attraction. Shakespeare reinforces this by having Juliet speak to the so-called friar:

DUKE: Love you the man that wronged you?

JULIET: Yes, as I love the woman that wronged him.

In their relationship, sexual desire is balanced with conscience in that they have shared a 'true contract' (I.ii.126) and are effectively married except for having a religious ceremony to bless their union (see **Contexts**: **Marriage law**, p. 69).

Paradoxically, the most lyrical description of their love is given to the unromantic Lucio:

Your brother and his lover have embraced;

As those that feed grow full, as blossoming time

That from the seedness the bare fallow brings

To teeming foison, even so her plenteous womb

Expresseth his full tilth and husbandry

(I.iv.40–4)

In the customers of Mistress Overdone's establishment, by contrast, the natural instinct of sexual desire has been indulged without any qualms of conscience, until they joke about the symptoms of sexually transmitted infections from which they all suffer. They do not speak of love, openly purchasing sex. Lucio, however, did promise marriage to Kate Keepdown in order to get her into bed. A gentleman would not propose marriage to a prostitute, and a prostitute would not need to be given this incentive to have sex with a gentleman. This implies that, like Juliet, she was virtuous, but, unlike Claudio, Lucio abandoned her when she fell pregnant and, her reputation in tatters, she seems to have had no one to turn to except Mistress Overdone. Lucio calls her a 'whore' and a 'punk', but it seems most likely that she only turned to prostitution after he rejected her. Just as Angelo defamed Mariana to give him an excuse to break his promise of marriage, so Lucio blackens Kate's reputation. Shakespeare seems to be suggesting that, because she was pregnant, he has forced her into prostitution. If Claudio were executed, this is the fate that might await Juliet, especially since her friends are unsympathetic and are withholding her dowry.

Balancing liberty and restraint

LUCIO: Why, how now, Claudio? Whence comes this restraint?

CLAUDIO: From too much liberty, my Lucio, liberty.

As surfeit is the father of much fast,

So every scope by the immoderate use

Turns to restraint.

(I.ii.106–110)

Build critical skills

Try exploring different interpretations of this speech by reading it aloud. Analyse the figurative language and discuss whether Lucio is using metaphor because he is embarrassed to be talking about sex to a nun, or whether he is mocking romantic poetry as being too sentimental for a 'man-about-town'.

Claudio is restrained in prison, and he blames too much freedom for his arrest. He suggests that, just as, after over-eating men fast for a while, so there will inevitably be a period of restraint after any over-indulgence. He argues that just as rats swallow poison of their own free will, so men will abuse their liberty and bring about their own destruction. The customers of Mistress Overdone's house of resort destroy their health in the pursuit of pleasure. The implication is that laws are needed to regulate human behaviour.

So, is restraint the answer? Isabella seeks a 'more strict restraint' (I.iv.4) than that offered by the convent of St Clare's, possibly thinking that she may fall into sin if given too much liberty, or possibly because she has romantic notion of self-sacrifice to prove her love of Christ. Isabella's self-restraint makes her put her chastity above the charity of saving her brother's life, and, instead of saintliness, this might appear as excessive self-regard. When Angelo broke his promise to marry her, Mariana restrained herself in a 'moated grange' (III.i.247), but this has had the reverse effect of making her love for Angelo more violent, as she spends her time brooding and listening to melancholy love songs. Angelo is another one who practises self-restraint, proudly saying, ''Tis one thing to be tempted, Escalus,/ Another thing to fall' (II.i.17–18). Like a rider controlling a spirited horse, Angelo holds his feelings in check. However, when once he gives his 'sensual race the rein' (II.iv.161) and releases his sexual desires, they are out of control; he finds himself having to resort to tyranny to have his way and to cover up his crimes.

The play shows that a balance needs to be found, but whether the final scene suggests that this balance has been found is open to interpretation. Even though Shakespeare has given Escalus a name which seems to be derived from the word 'scales', the most balanced character is arguably the Provost. The Provost has a position in the prison which is open to abuse, as the Duke recognises 'This is a gentle provost; seldom when/ The steeled gaoler is the friend of men' (IV.ii.73–4). The Provost manages to keep his oath and yet also show compassion and even try to change the deputy governor's mind. The Duke recognises his worth, thanks him for his 'care and secrecy' (V.i.522), and promises him promotion.

Appearance and reality

> ### TASK
> The whole plot is based on substitution.
> - List the obvious substitutions you can find where one person is substituted for another. Do you regard them as unnecessary deception or justifiable devices?
> - There are other, less obvious kinds of substitution, such as Elbow's malapropisms which are inappropriate. Do you think that there are other inappropriate substitutions such as the punishments meted out in the final scene?
> - Isabella asks Angelo to put himself in Claudio's position (II.ii.65–7). Who else suggests this imaginative substitution to Angelo?

The Duke and Mariana physically disguise their true identities, however, they think they are justified. As he explains the bed-trick to Isabella, the Duke, disguised as a friar, tells Isabella 'the doubleness of the benefit defends the deceit from reproof' (III.i.24–2), and he later explains in his soliloquy that 'Craft against vice I must apply' (III.ii.239) and Mariana's disguise is in a just cause: 'So disguise shall by th'disguised/ Pay with falsehood false exacting' (III.ii.242–3). As for his other deceptions, pretending to leave Vienna and substituting Ragozine's head for Claudio's, he claims in his final speech 'Th'offence pardons itself' (V.i.526).

The Duke's deceptions can possibly be excused by Machiavelli's maxim of 'the end justifies the means' (see **Contexts**, pp. 73–4), but Angelo's pretence is blatant hypocrisy, what Shakespeare calls 'seeming'. His name is, ironically, the opposite of what he is revealed to be, and in his first soliloquy, Shakespeare makes him say his name as he asks what he is: 'What dost thou or what art thou, Angelo?' (II.ii.177). The impression is given that he thought he was an 'angel' and is shocked to find out that he is not. His arrogant belief in himself as a saint is revealed a few lines later: 'Oh cunning enemy that, to catch a saint,/ With saints dost bait thy hook!' (II.ii.184–5).

The Duke already suspected that Angelo was not what he seemed: **'Hence shall we see/ If power change purpose, what our seemers be'** (I.iii.54–5). We later learn that he suspects Angelo because of his treatment of Mariana, but Angelo sets store by the law, not morality, and it was legal to break an engagement if the dowry could not be produced. Possibly, however, he did not want to appear materialistic, so that would explain why he defames her character. When Isabella realises what Angelo wants, she also accuses him of 'Seeming, seeming' (II.iv.151).

When Elbow tells the Duke, disguised as a friar, that Pompey is to go before the deputy, the Duke already knows about Angelo's vile proposition to Isabella, so he utters a rhyming couplet which sounds like a proverb meaning 'men should be what they seem': 'That we were all, as some would seem to be,/ From our faults, as faults from seeming, free' (III.ii.34–5). When Isabella pleads with the Duke in the final scene, she begs him not to judge by appearances:

> make not impossible
>
> That which but seems unlike. 'Tis not impossible
>
> But one, the wicked'st caitiff on the ground,
>
> May seem as shy, as grave, as just, as absolute
>
> As Angelo;

> > (V.i.51–4)

However, in order to expose Angelo, the Duke makes Isabella and even the friar appear truthful when they are not, and, to provoke Isabella's gratitude, he makes the Provost lie about Claudio's death. Lucio is also a practised pretender.

> **Top ten quotation**

TASK

Apart from the low-life characters, only Escalus and Claudio never pretend to be other than what they are. In his exploration of the theme of balance, how important is it for Shakespeare to have a character who is well-rounded, flawed, but a man of untarnished integrity?

Taking it further ▶▶

Watch this short discussion about the 2015 production by Cheek by Jowl. Which of the themes did this theatre company think were most important?

www.youtube.com/
watch?v=1SJcZtF4ZVM

Characters

Target your thinking

- How far does your response to the Duke colour your perception of the other characters? (**AO1**)
- What turning points can you identify for individual characters? (**AO2**)
- In what ways is Angelo more complex than a traditional stage villain? (**AO5**)

The Duke

▲ In 2004 at the Globe Theatre, Mark Rylance as Vincentio modelled himself on King James I

For most of the play, the Duke is an imposter. He adopts the disguise of a friar which gives him access to the private thoughts of everyone in Vienna, and he proceeds to act as a spy, even hiding to hear the conversation between Claudio and Isabella. He appoints as deputy a man he mistrusts in order to find out whether the virtuous Angelo is everything he seems, and, presumably, to find an opportunity to ensure that Angelo marries the jilted Mariana. The Duke brushes Angelo's own doubts aside and forces him into the position.

It is ironic that in order to expose Angelo as a seemer, the Duke himself becomes a seemer. His disguise makes people trust him and assume that he acts out of Christian motives, so even the Proctor goes against his better judgement and follows his directions. When the Duke learns of Angelo's treatment of Isabella, he could act openly, but he is determined that Angelo should not escape by arguing that he was just making trial of Isabella. He involves her in a plot which turns her into a seemer also. He makes her act against her principles, and lies to her so that she will be more eloquent and angry in her denunciation of Angelo. He even involves the friar in his scheming.

He pardons Claudio and asks for Isabella's hand in the same sentence, thus applying unfair emotional pressure. His Machiavellian tendencies are also revealed when he deliberately praises Angelo highly in order to lull him into a false sense of security. He even sends 'letters of strange tenor, perchance of the Duke's death, perchance entering into some monastery' (IV.ii.175–6), which might be calculated to excite Angelo's ambition and make him even more determined to try to hang on to his reputation.

However, Shakespeare shows that he is not totally successful as a Machiavellian ruler (see **Contexts**, pp. 73–4). He acknowledges that he has failed to assert control in his kingdom. He also fails to accept the responsibility for re-establishing order. He is too nervous to tell Mariana about the bed-trick, even though he told Isabella he would (III.i.239–40). He fails to realise that Angelo will not keep his bargain with Isabella. He does not anticipate that Barnadine will refuse to be executed; in fact, he was not aware that a prisoner has been in jail for nine years. He has been too reclusive and failed to keep in touch with his people so that all manner of scandalous rumours about him are spreading.

He changes his opinion to suit his motives. Pretending to be a friar, he tells Juliet that having intercourse with Claudio was a 'most offenceful act' (II.iii.26), and yet, so that he can trap Angelo, he advises Mariana that for her to lie with Angelo is no sin. It is only possible to distinguish between the cases with a legal quibble (see **Contexts: Marriage law**, p. 69). By showing mercy to everyone at the end, he undermines Angelo's attempts to re-impose Vienna's 'strict statutes and most biting laws' (I.iii.20), and this suggests that Shakespeare intended his primary motive for appointing Angelo to be to test him, not to restore order in the state.

Alternatively, it has been argued that he puts on religious robes in order to do good works and restore a harmonious balance to the state. A contemporary audience would have seen his friar's robes as symbolic of his status as God's representative on earth.

Build critical skills

Find evidence in the text which suggests that the Duke might be putting Isabella through excessively rigorous tests to assess her suitability as a wife.

Build critical skills

Does the end justify the means? What do you think Shakespeare is trying to achieve when he portrays the Duke testing Angelo by imposing the office of deputy on him? To what extent do you think Shakespeare wants audiences to agree with the Duke's actions?

CRITICAL VIEW

F.R. Leavis called the Duke 'a kind of Providence directing the action from above. His attitude *is* meant to be ours – his total attitude, which is the total attitude of the play' (*The Common Pursuit*, 1962, Peregrine Books). How far do you agree that the audience's attitude is meant to coincide with the Duke's?

The ending of the play might support this interpretation with three, or possibly four, marriages arranged, and all offences forgiven. It can be argued that he is, in a devious way, an influence for good, and the end justifies the means. When he lies to Claudio about Angelo's intentions and tells him he is to die, he does invite Claudio to come to an acceptance of death and ask forgiveness of Isabella. When he lies to Isabella about her brother's death, he gives her the opportunity to learn to show mercy.

The loyal Escalus describes him as 'One that above all other strifes contended especially to know himself' (III.ii.199), and there is evidence that he acquires self-knowledge as the story unfolds. At the beginning of the play, he scorned love; by the end he has realised that he can fall in love. At the beginning, he did not know his people and hid from them; by the end, he has learned about them first hand. His system of justice had been absolute, allowing no shades of grey: either release or execution (IV.ii.116), and he orders Barnadine's execution without qualm. However, when confronted with the condemned man, he realises that **'to transport him, in the mind he is,/ Were damnable'** (IV.iii.58–9).

Top ten quotation

The way in which the Duke's character is interpreted is the key to the reading of the whole play. In the Globe productions of 2004, he was even played as a floundering bungler who improvises as events go beyond his control so that the production could be a rollicking comedy for tourists to enjoy (see **Comedic structure**, pp. 45–6). This interpretation, however, is two-dimensional, and Shakespeare's Duke is far from that.

Taking it further ▶▶

Compare the presentation of the Duke in the blog of the director of the Globe and a review of a production at the Theatre Royal in Bath:

www.shakespearesglobe.com/discovery-space/adopt-an-actor/archive/vincentio-played-by-mark-rylance

www.bbc.co.uk/somerset/content/articles/2006/07/14/measure_for_measure_review_feature.shtml

CRITICAL VIEW

'We felt there must be this journey for the Duke and that … he comes to learn something about true government, about justice, about the entire system by which he has governed and lived. He now has to question all that.'

(Michael Pennington, *Shakespeare's Players*, edited by Judith Cook, 1983)

How far do you agree with this assessment of the Duke?

Isabella

Isabella is a novice of the order of St Clare, nuns who wear white to symbolise their chastity, so Shakespeare creates a stage picture in which Isabella appears visibly pure and virginal in the corrupt state of Vienna. Isabella is seen wishing there were even more restraint being asked of her. Like Angelo, she has a very clear view of morality and is reluctant to plead for her brother. She will have been taught to remain pure and chaste at any cost, like the Virgin Martyrs of the Catholic Church who underwent torture rather than yield their virginity.

Both Lucio and Angelo refer to her as a saint; she has devoted herself to the religious life and makes her moral decisions based on its teaching. To Angelo, she stresses the virtue of mercy; however, she is not confident that God will have mercy on her. When faced with an impossible dilemma, she falls back on what she has been taught, saying 'More than our brother is our chastity' (II.iv.186). When she hears of how Angelo has dishonoured Mariana, her response is similarly absolute: 'What a merit were it in death to take this poor maid from the world!' (III.i.219–20), putting herself in Mariana's shoes and stating what she would wish for herself. She refuses to compromise herself and her immortal soul. She tells the so-called friar, 'I have spirit to do any thing that appears not foul in the truth of my spirit' (III.i.197–8).

When a man the audience knows to be the secular Duke asks her to go to Angelo and appear to give in to his demands and then send another woman in her place, Shakespeare shows that she sees a way out of an impossible dilemma. She has been taught to obey religious authority, symbolised here by the holy friar. Similarly, when he asks her to lie to the Duke in the final scene, she trusts his judgement, even though she is reluctant to compromise her principles. Like Angelo, she learns that she should not think of herself as a saint; she should not be rigid and absolutist, but learn humility and exercise mercy.

Isabella is undoubtedly passionate, and she can be very cruel. Her last words to her brother suggest that their sibling rivalry has made their relationship uneasy. Indeed, Claudio's description of her to Lucio suggests that she was always able to get their father on her side. His assessment of her persuasiveness is shown to be justified in her two scenes with Angelo. She begins hesitantly but, as soon as her anger is aroused, she argues eloquently and does not give up until he turns away. Then her anger softens and she reverts to pleading, only leaving when she is given another appointment.

Each actor must decide how much awareness Isabella has of the effect she has on Angelo. Shakespeare gives her arguments which are carefully calculated to move him. She uses Christian doctrine to counter his legal argument; she attacks his pride and she challenges him to admit that he too has had similar thoughts. She introduces the idea of bribery; Shakespeare seems to be suggesting that she might be deliberately tempting Angelo, knowing how he will interpret that word.

When she returns next day, she does not understand what he is implying when he invites her to give up her body to 'sweet uncleanness'. When Angelo asks whether there might be charity in sin committed to save Claudio's life, she assumes he means the sin of pardoning a guilty man. When she eventually seems to understand what he is suggesting, she fancifully imagines herself undergoing torture to protect her virginity, but Shakespeare gives her the language of sado-masochistic sex, thus inflaming Angelo's lust still further.

It is possible to interpret Isabella as using such language unconsciously, thus revealing that she is also sexually attracted to Angelo without being aware of it. It is interesting to note that, in both Shakespeare's sources, the corrupt magistrate is married to the heroine at the end. Alternatively, she could be played as if she is deliberately using words, images and arguments which she knows will increase Angelo's desire for her. When he finally states his desire directly, instead of being shocked, she throws his honour back in his face and

Taking it further ▶

In both the 1994 BBC production of *Measure for Measure* and also in the Globe production in 2004, Isabella's final speech to Claudio in Act III, Scene i, lines 149–51 was omitted. How does this omission affect the interpretation of Isabella?

If you are lucky enough to watch or listen to a different production, listen carefully to see whether the text is manipulated.

Build critical skills

To what extent would you call Isabella the heroine of the play? Explain your answer using textual references. You may also refer to productions.

threatens to expose him if he does not pardon her brother. The speed with which she gives this ultimatum suggests that she is not as naïve as she appears and could have been deliberately manipulating him. If this was her plan, then it backfires, because she did not take into account the fact that he is a man with power and a reputation for integrity, while she is merely a woman, desperately trying any trick to save her brother's life.

CRITICAL VIEW

'I think she's scared. My Isabella was very frightened of sexuality. My Isabella was going to be a bride of Christ – that costume was actually her wedding dress.'

(Paola Dionisotti, *Clamorous Voices*, 1988)

How far do you think this interpretation fits with Isabella as Shakespeare has portrayed her?

CRITICAL VIEW

'The production – if its objective is that the audience should recognise Isabella's dilemma as opposed to merely observing her in critical detachment – has to support Isabella. Otherwise the audience will not really be challenged by the play; they'll have been let off the hook.'

(Juliet Stevenson, *Clamorous Voices*, 1988)

Do you agree that the production must support Isabella?

Angelo

The Duke sets the puritanical Angelo up to be the unpopular ruler in his absence so that he will be more popular on his return. Angelo, however, tries unsuccessfully to refuse the position. At first, through Lucio's descriptions, Angelo is perceived as cold and unnatural with 'snow-broth' instead of blood (I.iv.57–8) and urine of 'congealed ice' (III.ii.97). In his first conversation with Isabella, he reveals an ambition to act like a prophet and to use the law to eradicate 'future evils' (II.ii.98), whether existing or to be 'hatched and born' in the future (see **Puritanism,** p. 66).

CRITICAL VIEW

'In the case of Angelo, you are dealing with someone who is obviously a very efficient and competent career man but who knows nothing at all about himself sexually and is very much out of touch with that side of his personality. So that, when his sexuality is triggered off, it is of a very adolescent and uncertain kind.'

(Michael Pennington, *Shakespeare's Players*, edited by Judith Cook, 1983)

How far do you agree with this view?

Angelo's test comes from a surprising quarter. He had thought himself able to resist temptation but, as soon as he sees Isabella, he tells the Provost to stay, suggesting that he doubts his strength to resist the desire which is unexpectedly welling up. As Isabella warms up to her argument, Lucio urges her to 'touch him, there's the vein' (II.ii.72). He may well mean this literally. As she grows more passionate in her contempt for the arrogance of men, Lucio observes 'He's coming: I perceive't' (II.ii.129), another sexual reference which suggests that Angelo is no longer able to control his desire.

CRITICAL VIEW

'As Angelo … Rory Kinnear is outstanding. At first, he seems a shy bureaucrat astonished by his promotion. Once installed, he visibly grows in authority and then finds himself poleaxed when Isabella comes to plead for her brother's life. Where most Angelos are propelled by lust, Kinnear's is smitten by love: he sighs that Isabella may see him 'at any time' and studiously swaps his specs for contact lenses to make a good impression. This doesn't excuse the sexual bargain he proposes: what it does do is suggest that Angelo is a man floundering in unfamiliar emotional territory.'

(Michael Billington, reviewing the 2010 production at the Almeida Theatre)

Angelo turns defensive: 'Why do you put these sayings on me?' (II.ii.137) and then admits in an aside that he does desire Isabella: 'She speaks, and 'tis such sense/ That my sense breeds with it.' Abruptly he turns to go, putting himself out of reach of temptation, but she begs him to turn back, offering to bribe him. She has renounced worldly goods, so, in his current state of mind, he must be thinking that she is offering to bribe him with her body. (For analysis of his soliloquies, see **Soliloquies**, pp. 48–9.)

He is so convinced of his own moral superiority that he questions whether his feelings are her fault, whether the tempter is as guilty as the one who allows himself to be tempted. He struggles all night with his feelings, but he can no longer pray to be delivered from temptation when, more than anything else at this moment, he wants to give in to it. He knows that what he wants is evil, but he cannot stop himself; he believes he is already damned just because he desires her (see **Puritanism**, p. 66).

Angelo is reluctant to lose the sense of superiority that made him smile 'when men were fond', and he takes pride in his reputation for gravity. It is this pride that is his worst sin because, in order to preserve his reputation, he decides to use Claudio's life as a lever to persuade Isabella to give herself to him, thinking that no one will believe her word against his. Having made this decision and given his 'sensual race the rein' (II.iv.161), he is then forced further into vice. Isabella resists and threatens him with exposure, so he warns her that he will 'prove a tyrant' (II.iv.170) and order Claudio to be tortured. From this point, there is no turning back, and, in order to preserve his reputation, he is forced to order

CRITICAL VIEW

A psychoanalytic critic would judge that Angelo has a highly developed super-ego, meaning that he believes he is impervious to temptation. However, his id, representing his inner desires, is powerfully awakened by Isabella, and, unwilling to lose his reputation, he bullies Isabella into giving in to him, rather than proposing to her openly.

Claudio's early execution to avoid a revenge attack. As he realises in his third soliloquy, 'Alack, when once our grace we have forgot,/ Nothing goes right: we would, and we would not.' (IV.v.31–2)

Taking it further ▶

Watch this scene starring David Tennant from a 2008 documentary about presenting Shakespeare today:

www.youtube.com/
watch?v=uz4_ec5DMgA

How does David Tennant interpret Angelo and his feelings for Isabella?

Why do you think the actor kept his natural accent?

Like Macbeth and Othello, he has the potential to be a good leader of men; Escalus says of him:

> If any in Vienna be of worth
>
> To undergo such ample grace and honour
>
> It is Lord Angelo.
>
> (I.i.22–4)

At the end, Escalus reinforces the tragedy (see p. 22) of Angelo's fall:

> I am sorry one so learned and so wise
>
> As you, Lord Angelo, have still appeared,
>
> Should slip so grossly,
>
> (V.i.467–9)

and this provokes a parallel speech from Angelo, craving death as his just punishment. Angelo, however, also has a tragic flaw. Like Iago and the witches, the Duke manipulates Angelo instead of allowing him to come to greater self-knowledge naturally. Why, then, is Angelo not perceived as a tragic hero? (See p. 23) Perhaps, if Shakespeare had allowed him to kill himself when exposed, instead of demanding 'Immediate sentence then, and sequent death' (V.i.366), the audience's feelings would be different, but Shakespeare has him treated as a pawn by the Duke, allowing him few words in the final scene. Some may think it wrong that Angelo escapes official punishment; however, for Angelo to be forced to live with his guilt and his destroyed reputation is a far greater punishment than death.

Shakespeare was not writing a tragedy; he has written a play about balance, and Mariana may have the answer when she says:

> They say best men are moulded out of faults,
>
> And for the most become much more the better
>
> For being a little bad: so may my husband.
>
> (V.i.432–4)

Top ten quotation ▷

He has been offered redemption; Shakespeare does not tell whether he accepts it.

CRITICAL VIEW

'I felt very strongly that Angelo's crime is not what he thinks it is. He thinks it is desiring a saint, whereas it is a political crime; it is a monstrous abuse of his position, so that I think the crux of his downfall is political.'

(Michael Pennington, *Shakespeare's Players*, edited by Judith Cook, 1983)

How far do you agree with this actor's interpretation?

Lucio

Lucio is a gentleman, but also 'a fantastic', dressed extravagantly to draw attention to himself. His name means 'light', which is appropriate for someone with his lightweight morals and his light, easy wit, ever ready to rise up and prick the bubble of hypocrisy. The audience laugh with him but also at him, especially if the actor plays him as being embarrassed at talking about sex with Isabella, a virtuous woman. He usually speaks in prose, so his attempt at romantic poetry can be portrayed as amusing.

He pretends to have inside knowledge about the élite of Viennese society and boasts that he is an 'inward' of the Duke. The audience appreciates the dramatic irony as he slanders the Duke to Friar Lodowick, and the friar to the Duke, waiting eagerly for Lucio to find out that they are the same person. At the end of the play, he sabotages the Duke's carefully planned scene in which he hopes to play the benign ruler, restoring harmony to the city, earning the gratitude of all, especially Isabella. Instead, the Duke is revealed to be a petty little man, magnanimously pardoning everyone except Lucio. He declares that 'slandering a prince' is unpardonable, the worst crime.

However, Lucio is introduced as a cynical lecher who has 'purchased' many diseases under Mistress Overdone's roof. He makes jokes about the obviously very familiar symptoms and cures for syphilis. Shakespeare makes him quick-witted and clever with words, as in the **antithetical** 'I had as lief have the foppery of freedom as the morality of imprisonment'. He confidently bandies words with a bawd, or a friar, or a duke. He sees sex as 'a game of tick-tack', women as sexual playthings, and nothing wrong in promising marriage to Kate Keepdown, getting her pregnant and then abandoning her. He seems to have informed against Mistress Overdone and Pompey to the authorities, and he callously refuses to help Pompey. He epitomises the amoral spirit of Viennese society under the Duke.

It seems that Shakespeare uses this character in various ways, and they do not always fit together. Lucio is a close and loyal friend to Claudio, working hard for his release. He persuades Isabella to plead with Angelo, gives her confidence and coaches her in how she can best use her talents to move Angelo. However, Shakespeare presents him as a total contrast to the virtuous Claudio. Lucio places Isabella on a pedestal 'as a thing enskied or sainted', because she is a pure woman waiting to enter the nunnery. However, he attacks a friar, a man of God, physically, because Shakespeare needs someone to expose the Duke's identity in an act which symbolises the intrigue and pretence being stripped away. Nevertheless, in the theatre these contradictions are not apparent; the audience can just enjoy Lucio for the colour and light he brings to a play which only just misses being a tragedy.

Taking it further

If you have been lucky enough to see a production of the play, consider how Lucio was portrayed. Has he been used merely to provide comedy, or have sinister aspects of his character been brought out?

antithesis: contrast of ideas expressed by balancing words or phrases of opposite meaning.

Claudio

Claudio is the necessary focus of the play's debate about abstract concepts such as justice and mercy. However, Shakespeare makes him a fully rounded character; perhaps the only one in the play with whom an audience can identify.

Mistress Overdone, Escalus and the Provost all speak highly of him, and his friend, Lucio, who says that Claudio always keeps his promises, is moved to extraordinary efforts to effect his release. He is a law-abiding citizen, not questioning the justice of his arrest, only the public humiliation. The audience is immediately on his side; he is faithful to the woman he loves, and she loves him enough to stand up to the so-called friar and declare her lack of regret and her sadness that she is not to be executed with him. Claudio and Juliet may be minor characters, but they are the only ones who understand what love really is.

When the so-called friar visits him in prison, Claudio is humble and appears to be comforted by the Duke's long homily; however, as soon as Isabella enters, we realise he is still hoping for a reprieve. He bravely declares that he will 'encounter darkness as a bride/ And hug it in mine arms' (III.i.83–4), but, being human, the fact that there is a way to avoid death encourages him to cling to that hope and try to persuade Isabella to save him. His speech about death is one of the most powerful in the play: '… **to die and go we know not where,/ To lie in cold obstruction and to rot …**'. The sympathetic way in which Claudio is presented in this scene may harden the audience's feelings against Isabella, whose last words to her condemned brother are likely to be viewed as unbelievably cruel.

> **Top ten quotation** ⟶

Escalus

Escalus is an experienced statesman whose name symbolises a balance of judgement. Unlike Angelo, in Escalus, justice is tempered with mercy; he is aware that we are all potential sinners. He is a well-rounded character, roused to anger when the so-called friar calls the Duke unjust, but he has a human side to him and enjoys Pompey's wit, obviously understanding the sexual innuendo. He lets Pompey off with a warning, although he is probably too lenient as Pompey's aside shows that he has no intention of reforming. Escalus is loyal to the Duke, but the Duke does not involve him in his schemes so Shakespeare is able to present him as a standard of honour and integrity in a corrupt world.

The Provost

The Provost, an officer charged with the apprehension, custody and punishment of offenders, is a kind man. He has been lenient in his treatment of Barnadine, and he speaks up for Claudio. He takes his oath seriously, but, once he is convinced that the friar speaks with the authority of the Duke, he helps keep Claudio alive and suggests the substitution of Ragozine's head.

Mariana

Mariana is essential to the plot, but she is unlikely to engage the audience's sympathy. After Angelo's rejection of her, she cut herself off from society. She trusts the so-called friar, who seems to have been visiting her in disguise for a long while; she follows his advice in a risky plot to entrap Angelo. When the Duke makes Angelo marry her to reinstate her reputation, he tests her love by offering her Angelo's possessions after his execution to buy a better husband. She proves her love and faith in Angelo, but the marriage is unlikely to be a happy one, although her name suggests a reference to the Virgin Mary, indicating that she might have a redemptive function.

Pompey

Pompey is a barman and a pimp, procuring prostitutes for men's pleasure. However, he provides much of the humour as he is clever, witty and irreverent. He is never at a loss for a witty riposte, as when he tells Barnadine, who pleads that he is not ready to be hanged as he is drunk and sleepy, that he will sleep more soundly after being hanged. When Pompey is arrested and brought before Escalus, the audience enjoys the clever way in which he manages to emerge the victor from his interrogation. He is an accomplished stand-up comedian who appears to improvise as he makes fun of the audience, whom he casts as fellow prisoners. Shakespeare also gives him important contributions to the main themes. Pompey points out that laws are man-made and not necessarily based on justice, so they can be changed, and also that laws do not change human behaviour nor cure human weakness.

Mistress Overdone

Her name is a pun on the verb 'do', being a slang term for sex, suggesting that she is a worn-out prostitute. She owns the brothel and inherited her name when she married her ninth husband. She gives a succinct summary of the state of Vienna when she bemoans the loss of trade: 'What with the war, what with the sweat, what with the gallows, and what with poverty, I am custom-shrunk.'

Writer's methods: Form, structure and language

Target your thinking

- How has Shakespeare made use of soliloquies and asides in this play? (**AO2**)
- How important is knowledge of the coins that were used in Shakespeare's day? (**AO3**)
- How can Shakespeare's use of dramatic irony lead to different interpretations for the characters and the audience? (**AO5**)

Structure

TASK

Make a chart comparing Crane's act and scene divisions with Shakespeare's own.

Taking it further ▶

When you reached the end of Act II the first time you watched or read the play, what did you think was going to happen in the end?

Shakespeare did not think in terms of a five-act structure; this was imposed by Ralph Crane, who produced transcripts of plays for the King's Men, when he wrote out a copy of the play for the *First Folio*, the collected edition of Shakespeare's plays printed in 1623. Shakespeare structured his play in scenes which came to an end when all the actors left the stage. So the playwright's intended structure was 16 scenes.

In the first half of the play, until the Duke emerges from the hiding place where he has been listening to Isabella and Claudio, the Duke is an observer. Vienna is in a state of anarchy and, in his attempts to bring back order, Angelo is merciless, interpreting the law rigorously without any attempt to temper justice with mercy, and then he gives his 'sensual race the rein' (II.iv.161), and abandons all 'decorum'.

In the second half of the play the Duke is galvanised into action by the conversation he has overheard. Speaking in business-like prose rather than verse, he takes back control and sets in motion a scheme to expose Angelo. After her painful outburst at Claudio, which was overheard by the so-called friar, Isabella is much more subdued and less assertive, accepting the so-called friar's directions. Shakespeare brings in Mariana who is able to re-establish harmony because she can legitimately give herself to Angelo since the consummation of their earlier contract makes her his wife. Without his knowledge, she saves him from the sin of fornication. She also saves him from the punishment for his intent to murder Claudio through her pleas to the Duke and her ability to persuade Isabella to join her. This also saves Isabella who, with Mariana's help, learns forgiveness and the importance of tempering justice with mercy.

The structure is based around secret identities and the Duke's manipulation of people and events. The Duke disguises himself as a friar, and then he masterminds two other secret plans involving mistaken identity: he persuades Mariana to take Isabella's place, and he persuades the Provost to send the head of a dead pirate in place of Claudio's. This complex plot is only resolved when the Duke's identity is revealed.

Comedic structure

The structure of *Measure for Measure* may be seen as moving from a state of chaos in Vienna to a harmonious conclusion. At the beginning, **'Liberty plucks Justice by the nose'** and the Duke is running away from his responsibilities; at the end, the Duke returns and takes up the reins of government, righting wrongs and restoring order. As in Shakespeare's comedies there is confusion, caused by mistaken identities, deception and disguise, which leads to twists and turns in the plot before the plays end happily and lovers are reunited.

> **Top ten quotation**

CRITICAL VIEW

'Playing Measure for Measure *as a comedy was a bit of a risk; over the last fifty years, the play's tragedy has been emphasised more frequently than the humour, but we thought "It's been written down as a comedy, so maybe we should just trust that that's what Shakespeare wanted it to be" … we tried to play the story as a thriller, full of well-laid plans that go slightly awry but come good eventually.'*

(Transcription from Mark Rylance's podcast, Globe production, 2004)

In the Globe's production, Mark Rylance played the Duke and, at the beginning of Act I, Scene iii, he was carried on stage hidden in a laundry basket. This was intended to explain how he escaped secretly to the friary instead of travelling to Poland, as he said he would. As he stood up, he was festooned with women's underwear, suggesting to Friar Thomas and the audience that 'the dribbling dart of love' had got him into a sticky situation.

Productions that decide to bring out the comedy have plenty of material. The Duke's preoccupation with 'back-wounding calumny' can easily make him a figure of fun, as well as the fact that he often seems to be clutching at straws and sometimes his plans go awry, as when he is reduced to beseeching Barnadine to allow himself to be executed. He is not one of the comic characters, but can be played humorously, as Mark Rylance demonstrates in his podcasts.

The structure puts the Duke at the centre of *Measure for Measure*, and the audience focuses on him throughout the play, most of which he spends in disguise as a friar. The opening scene is a formal public scene dealing with the hasty departure of the Duke and his appointment of Angelo as deputy in his absence. The final scene is the only other public scene and there are interesting parallels between the two. Once again the Duke abruptly withdraws, without an explanation, and Angelo is given another commission – to investigate the accusations made against him. The appointment of Angelo in the first scene leads to him becoming a rigorous and ruthless ruler, revealing him to be a hypocrite. In the final scene, Angelo's appointment allows the Duke to come on in disguise and provide the traditional ending for a comedy in which the villain is exposed, and the play ends with mercy, forgiveness and marriages.

Build critical skills

Do you think the play needs stage business such as this in order to raise laughs, or are the situations, the characters and the dialogue funny enough on their own?

Shakespeare's comedies show that love conquers all, and the love of Claudio and Juliet, who are finally reunited, is even stronger for having been tested. Mariana's devotion is rewarded and she is married to Angelo, although Angelo's last words are to beg for death. However, as his loyal wife asserts, he may **'become much more the better/ For being a little bad'**. All ends well for Kate Keepdown who marries the father of her child, although Lucio regards this as a punishment worse than death. Finally, there is the possibility of a marriage between the Duke and Isabella.

Top ten quotation

However, in his comedies, Shakespeare gives all the information the audience needs to assess the characters as early as possible. The structure he has chosen for *Measure for Measure* means that the audience has to re-evaluate their judgement of characters as the play progresses. In this play, Shakespeare withholds information at the beginning and essential facts are only revealed later. In Act III, we realise that the Duke does not want to test Angelo so much as expose him as a hypocrite and rectify the injustice done to Mariana. It is not until half way through the play that the Duke gives details of the 'kind of character' in Angelo's life, 'That to th'observer doth thy history/ Fully unfold', of which he spoke in the first scene; however, when he spoke the words, the audience was not aware that he was speaking ambiguously. Importantly, not until Act IV, Scene ii does Shakespeare reveal that the sacrifice demanded of Isabella would have been futile, as Angelo intends to have Claudio executed whether or not Isabella submits to him.

The subplot

The characters and action of the subplot can be seen as parallel to the main plot. Claudio is arrested under the sudden revival of neglected laws concerning morality, and so are Pompey and Mistress Overdone. Angelo is the law enforcer in the main plot, Elbow in the subplot. Comic scenes are used to present an ironic commentary on the serious scenes of the main plot, but the subplot is not fully developed. Shakespeare does not give the low-life characters a full storyline so they are mainly used to provide comic relief from the potential tragedy that constitutes the main plot.

Although the minor characters embody the corruption in Vienna, nevertheless they are witty and sympathetic, suggesting that Shakespeare did not intend them to be held up as examples of how not to behave.

Juxtaposition

Shakespeare often juxtaposes contrasting scenes to achieve a particular effect. The play opens with a formal scene in blank verse, in which the Duke, Escalus and Angelo speak of justice, virtue and honour. This is juxtaposed with three syphilitic libertines, speaking in prose, hoping that the Duke does not make a treaty because they like the opportunities for plunder offered in war, and laughing about their symptoms and the fact that they never go to church.

Shakespeare succinctly demonstrates the problems in Vienna and the need for remedy. The Duke's Machiavellian plotting at the end of Act I, Scene iii, is highlighted by being immediately followed by the virtuous Isabella.

In Act II, Scene i, Angelo and Escalus are discussing justice, the law and Claudio's impending execution. Escalus piously asks heaven to forgive Claudio and 'us all', and then Shakespeare brings on the comic characters to demonstrate how the law actually functions in Vienna. The ridiculous Elbow, who tries to use long words and fails hilariously, is the representative of the law; Pompey runs rings round Elbow, and he manages to persuade Escalus to let him off with a caution, which, as he tells the audience in an aside, he plans to ignore. The law as it stands is ineffective, but who in the audience will agree with the death penalty for Claudio?

Shakespeare creates verbal echoes to point the irony. The Duke observes that 'Lord Angelo is precise' (I.iii.51), meaning puritanical, and Elbow mistakenly affirms that Pompey and Froth are 'precise villains ... void of all profanation in the world that good Christians ought to have' (II.i.51–2). By the end of Act II, Angelo really is a precise villain, but the audience has already been warned not to be taken in by his professions of piety.

In Act IV, Scene iii, Shakespeare juxtaposes a witty comic routine with the Duke learning one of the most serious lessons about being a judge. He comes to realise that it would be damnable for both the condemned man and the judge to execute him unprepared to meet his Maker. With this revelation and the Duke's plans to bring events to a head, Shakespeare juxtaposes the Duke's lie to Isabella that her brother is dead and her violent and aggressive reaction to this betrayal. He prevents the scene ending on a tragic note, however, by bringing on Lucio with his slanderous stories about the Duke, which reduce the latter to a powerless protester.

Dramatic devices

Soliloquies and asides

The Duke

The Duke's soliloquy at Act III, Scene ii, lines 223–44 is separated from the play by being composed in rhyming couplets of lines of eight syllables. Instead of revealing his turbulent emotions, however, the Duke sounds like a Chorus observing in a detached manner that he has to bear a heavy burden as God's deputy on earth and explaining why he is having to use 'craft against vice'.

The Duke also has a short soliloquy (III.ii.158–61) in which he expresses his outrage at Lucio's 'back-wounding calumny'. In Act IV, Scene i, while Isabella and Mariana 'walk aside', Shakespeare gives him a short aside which reveals that he is still brooding on his vulnerability to false rumours. In view of the

Build critical skills

Does Shakespeare give the audience any insights into the Duke from his soliloquy in Act IV, Scene iii, lines 98–102?

hazardous venture on which he has embarked, playing with the trust of both Mariana and Isabella, this concern seems remarkably petty and selfish.

In Act IV, Scene iii, lines 84–92, Shakespeare reveals the Duke's plans as he utters his thoughts aloud; however, the speech does not give any insights into his feelings.

The only time when we seem to be given access to the Duke's inner feelings is actually when he is talking to Claudio in disguise as a friar (III.i.5–41). In this speech he is addressing life, using the second person pronouns 'thee' and 'thou', possibly emulating the Bible to make his speech sound like a sermon, but possibly to show his contempt for life which, he says, is 'death's fool', not 'noble' nor 'valiant'. He puts forward a series of examples and images which argue that life is not worth living. He is not speaking as one would expect of a Christian friar to a condemned man; there is no mention of repentance or heaven.

CRITICAL VIEW

"I found that if I related the lines to myself as much as to Claudio the speech was unlocked for me, and a central part of the Duke's character fell into place. His sense of self has fragmented into "many a thousand grains" of dust … In a sense the purpose of the Duke's journey through the play so far is to realise completely his own sceptical fatalism. But somehow this can only be expressed through someone else's situation.'

(Roger Allam, *Players of Shakespeare 3*, 1994)

In this speech, how far do you think Shakespeare intends the Duke to be trying to sound like a friar, and how far thinking aloud?

Angelo

By contrast, Angelo has three heart-searching soliloquies that give valuable insights into his character and why he behaves as he does. In Act II, Scene ii, he has two brief asides which give the audience an inkling of what is happening to him, followed by a soliloquy in which Shakespeare manages to make him sound shocked that he has been assailed so suddenly and so devastatingly by sexual desire. Questions, mid-line **cæsurae**, non-verbal exclamations and repetition all help to show his confusion. He even debates whether Isabella is to blame for tempting him. His arrogance is seen in the fishing metaphor of using a saint to catch a saint! He is convinced that he has only been tempted because she is a modest and virtuous woman, and horrified that he should think of corrupting a nun.

cæsura: a pause in a line of verse.

This scene ends with Angelo, and, as he is still wrestling with his feelings at the beginning of Scene iv, Shakespeare gives the impression that Angelo has been agonising all night.

chiasmus: see p. 21.

Shakespeare uses an example of **chiasmus** ('…pray and think, I think and pray') to emphasise that, while he tries to pray to heaven, his thoughts are with Isabella. As he speaks to God in heaven, his words stay in his mouth, while in his heart are thoughts of 'swelling evil', an erotic image. He admits that he puts on a false face of modesty, hoping that no one will hear him say he takes pride in his 'gravity', his dignified presence. He wants to control his desires but cannot, and he realises that 'false seeming' must now govern his behaviour. When Isabella is announced, he struggles to control the quickening of his blood. He appeals to heaven, but Shakespeare uses two similes to graphically describe how he feels that his heart is being suffocated by his blood. Heart-searching cannot help if the racing of his blood prevents him from listening to his heart.

In his final soliloquy (IV.iv.18–32), he speaks of 'the deed' because it seems the killing of Claudio and the violation of Isabella are inseparable in his mind. The unconscious sexual innuendo of 'unshapes me', 'eminent body' and 'enforced' reveals how deeply disturbed he is. He worries that Isabella might expose him, but decides that she will not dare challenge his reputation. He feels deep regret for the execution of Claudio, progressing from 'He should have lived' to 'Would yet he had lived'. Like Macbeth, he realises that one mistake leads to horrifying consequences.

These soliloquies give Angelo the potential to develop as a tragic figure (see p. 23), but he is not given another opportunity to show his thoughts, so after this the audience sees only the front that he shows to the world and not his inner turmoil.

Isabella

Isabella has only one soliloquy at the end of Act II, Scene iv. Unlike Angelo, she does not struggle with her conscience but comes to an absolute certainty. If the 'perilous mouth' who is condemning her brother to death for fornication is now asking her to commit the same sin, there can be no justice because the judge himself is corrupt. There is no hope. However, her hyperbolic assurance that, if Claudio had 20 heads he would yield them up before allowing his sister to be defiled, betrays the lack of confidence in his opinion that she reveals in Act III, Scene i, line 73. The short line at line 184 allows the actor to pause and push doubt aside before she comes to her decision, which she states in rhyming couplets to reinforce her resolve.

Her antithetical statement balancing life and death, herself and her brother: 'Isabel live chaste, and brother die' may seem unbelievably harsh to a modern audience. However, she avoids using the first person pronoun 'I', using instead her name and then the plural pronoun 'our'. At this crisis, she falls back on what she has been taught as a novice. This is a formal statement of the belief which she has been taught as she prepared to become a nun. How do you weigh someone else's life against your own immortal soul? Her instructors have told to choose death over dishonour and she applies this teaching to a situation for which she has not been prepared.

This soliloquy does not reveal Isabella's true nature, but it clearly explains her dilemma.

This speech reveals Isabella's horror and naivety, but Shakespeare distances the audience from her thoughts as events unfold and she matures, so she does not

Context

One of the basic principles of medieval medicine was that of the four humours of which a human body was composed. The balance between these four (blood, phlegm, yellow bile, and black bile) was essential for the well-being of a person. Angelo thinks that he is suffering from an excess of blood, preventing him from responding rationally.

Build critical skills

At this crisis in her life, why do you think Shakespeare does not show Isabella praying to her God?

Build critical skills

At this point in the play, how do you respond to Shakespeare's presentation of Isabella and her beliefs?

TASK

Explore other ways in which the Duke's true identity could have been revealed.

Why do you think Shakespeare chose to have him exposed in this humorous manner?

evoke the sympathy another soliloquy might have generated. Had she been the focus of the play, a soliloquy in the second half would have revealed her feelings after her cruel verbal attack on her brother and how she felt about the supposed friar's plots and the part he expected her to play.

Disguise

The Duke disguises himself as a friar; that means he wears a long habit with a loose hood which can be pulled forward to cover his face. It also means that people from all walks of life will trust him with confessions, and value his advice. His disguise leads to a lot of dramatic irony as the audience knows his true identity but, of the other characters, only the friar knows. The humour of this disguise is exploited to the full with Lucio who slanders the Duke to the friar and then the friar to the Duke, so the audience eagerly anticipates what will happen when the Duke reveals himself.

One particular piece of irony is when Lucio says '*Cucullus non facit monachum*, honest in nothing but his clothes' (V.i.260–1); the Latin translates as 'The cowl does not make the monk', a proverbial phrase which is very apt, but reveals that he clearly has not rumbled the disguise! With a clever twist, it is actually Lucio who reveals the friar's true identity, and in doing so he reveals his own pretence to be an 'inward' or intimate friend of the Duke (III.ii.114).

In the final scene, Mariana appears wearing a veil, and so disguising her identity. Angelo expects to unmask 'a strange abuse' when he commands 'let's see thy face' (V.i.202), but ironically, what he actually reveals is his own hypocrisy, his broken promise of marriage five years before, and the woman who testifies that he had sexual intercourse with her instead of Isabella.

Irony

Shakespeare keeps the audience on the edge of their seats and thinking about the issues raised in the play with the use of irony, in which an apparently straightforward statement or event is undermined by its context so as to give it a very different significance. Dramatic irony is when the audience knows something other characters do not, such as the identity of Friar Lodowick, and this leads to a lot of humour, especially at the expense of Lucio.

Another kind of irony is when a character says something, which later turns out to be true, such as when Angelo unwittingly condemns himself to death with the boast:

> When I that censure him do so offend,
>
> Let mine own judgement pattern out my death,
>
> And nothing come in partial
>
> (II.i.29–31)

Top ten quotation

Angelo understands the unconscious irony of Isabella's conventional polite phrases, and his asides point the irony for the audience. When she leaves saying

'Save your honour' (II.ii.166), she is using 'honour' as a synonym for 'lordship', but he responds by referring to the other meaning, hoping that he can save his honour from his dishonourable attraction to her. Similarly when she asks 'I am come to know your pleasure' (II.iv.31), she is merely asking why he asked her to return. He picks up on the other meaning and replies that it would please him if she understood what he wanted without him having to spell it out for her.

To Isabella, Lucio describes Angelo as 'one who never feels/ The wanton stings and motions of the sense' (I.iv.58–9). The audience may remember this line when Angelo is suffering 'the wanton stings and motions of the sense', ironically provoked by Isabella.

Setting and atmosphere

Strict censorship prevented playwrights from making direct comments about the king or the state, and since the dissolution of the monasteries, there had been no friaries or nunneries in England, a strictly Protestant country. Shakespeare therefore set his play in the city-state of Catholic Vienna. However, there are no details in the play which suggest that Shakespeare's Vienna is based on the actual city. In his depiction of the corrupt underbelly of Vienna, he seems to be writing about the London with which he was familiar. Like London, the suburbs of Vienna are a hotbed of sexual depravity, because it was more difficult to regulate brothels outside the city limits.

Vienna is portrayed as a city of extremes. Six of the scenes are set in the corridors of power, three in religious houses, one in Mariana's 'moated grange'. However, four are set in the prison, one in a brothel and some of the disreputable characters are brought to the court. The atmosphere of most of the scenes is quite claustrophobic, as many of them are set in confined spaces such as the prison, a nunnery and Mariana's grange, which is surrounded by a moat instead of a wall. The final scene, however, is public by a 'consecrated fount/ A league below the city' (IV.iii.89–90).

Patterns of imagery

Clothing

Reflecting the extremes of settings, Shakespeare has chosen to place Isabella in an order which requires its adherents to wear white, symbolising purity and virginity, whereas the friars and Angelo are probably wearing black, symbolising their puritanical outlook on life. At first, many of the characters see things in black and white, but they learn to compromise: chastity needs to be tempered with charity, justice with mercy. They learn that faith must not be allowed to overreach into fanaticism, nor control into tyranny; mercy should not decline into leniency, nor love into lust.

Since the low-life characters represent the corruption and depravity in the city, costume designers can allow their imaginations free rein and offer a riot of

---

Context

In September 1603, James I ordered the property in London's suburbs inhabited by 'dissolute and idle persons' to be demolished to prevent the spread of the plague. Not surprisingly, many of the brothels were pulled down.

Taking it further

Watch this short trailer for an American production of the play. How well chosen are the images and settings included?

www.youtube.com/watch?v=aIMapfvRthc

---

colour to contrast with the characters in the main plot. Lucio, described in the character list as 'a fantastic', would be wearing extravagant colours, allying him with the world of the brothel, but, as a gentleman, his clothes would reflect the most extreme fashions of the time.

The sober friar's habit worn by the Duke appears to the other characters to be a symbol of holiness, but the audience know that it is a ruse, enabling the Duke to spy on his subjects. Throughout the play, Shakespeare uses images of clothing to suggest pretence. At the beginning, the Duke tells Escalus that Angelo will only be **'dressed'** with the Duke's love; Angelo will appear to be the Duke's substitute, but in reality the Duke has no intention of leaving the state with Angelo in charge.

Shakespeare employs imagery from clothes and the external trappings of power when Isabella argues that what **'great ones'** wear or carry to symbolise their authority is not as important as **'mercy'** (II.ii.60–4). Later in the scene she contemptuously points out that 'man, proud man,/ Dressed in a little brief authority … Plays such fantastic tricks before high heaven/ As makes the angels weep' (II.ii.121–6); the power of which men are so proud is only lent them for a short while, and they should remember this and wield it with heavenly grace and mercy. In his soliloquy, Angelo recognises that his outward appearance of moral rectitude – enhanced by his black clothes, his puritanical 'habit' – (II.iv.12–15) deceives everyone. By the final scene, however, Isabella seeks to expose the fact that Angelo's 'dressings' (V.i.56) conceal an 'arch-villain'.

Horse riding

Shakespeare uses riding a horse as a metaphor for controlling the populace, as well as an image of keeping sexual desire under control. When the Duke tells the friar the reasons for his disguise, he speaks of his subjects as 'headstrong' horses who need 'bits and curbs' (I.iii.21); however, in a revealing mixed metaphor, he uses 'weeds' instead of 'steeds', suggesting utter contempt for those who are unable to discipline themselves.

Claudio compares the 'body public', the population of Vienna, with a horse and Angelo with its new rider, saying that, to assert his authority, he 'lets it straight feel the spur' (I.ii.140–3). In the light of what happens later, this image could also represent Angelo holding his animal desires in check. When Angelo decides that he has gone too far to turn back, incriminating himself in his approaches to Isabella, he gives his 'sensual race the rein' (II.iv.161). His sexual desires are compared with a stallion which has been released from the rider's control to follow its instincts.

> **Top ten quotation**

> **Top ten quotation**

> **Build critical skills**
>
> Explore the symbolism of Mariana's veil in the final scene.

Context

'Give a wild horse the liberty of his head never so little and he will run headlong to thine and his own destruction also … So correct children in their tender years.'

(Phillip Stubbes, *The Anatomy of Abuses*, 1587)

Coins

When the Duke tells Angelo that he is to be appointed deputy, Angelo likens himself to a metal coin that should be tested for its value and worth: 'Before so noble and so great a figure/ Be stamp'd upon it' (I.i.49–50). In the sixteenth century, the value stamped on the coin was equal to the value of the metal used in its making, so he feels he should be tested to be sure he can live up to the task.

The angel-noble was a gold coin bearing the image of the Archangel Michael defeating Satan in the form of a dragon. Angelo seems to feel that, like the Archangel, he should actively destroy the evil which infects the state, and so he takes the severe measure of sentencing someone to death for fornication. The Duke used the same metaphor from coinage before Angelo entered, asking Escalus: 'What **figure** of us think you he will bear?' (I.i.16).

At the beginning of Angelo's second interview with Isabella, he exclaims against 'these filthy vices', declaring it would be like pardoning a murderer to pardon someone who fathered a child out of wedlock, who did:

> … coin heaven's image
>
> In stamps that are forbid. 'Tis all as easy
>
> Falsely to take away a life true made
>
> As to put metal in restrainèd means
>
> To make a false one.

(II.iv.44–8)

According to the Bible, God made man in his own image, and Angelo compares fathering an illegitimate child, which would also be made in God's image, with stamping a counterfeit coin, both of which crimes were punishable by death. Even as he plans to coerce Isabella into having sex with him, he expresses his disgust at what he is about to do. Isabella later tells him that women are 'credulous to false prints' (line 131), showing that she understands that women are easily persuaded by counterfeit persuasion.

Angelo seems to think that Isabella is here admitting that she is weak and ready to give into him. However, is there a suggestion that Isabella does not include herself in this general admission, thinking that, as a novitiate nun, she is distanced from, or even above, other women?

Escalus uses the language of coins when he tells Angelo that he is sorry that 'one so learned and so wise … Should slip so grossly' (V.i.463–5). In Shakespeare's time a 'slip' was a counterfeit coin, so Shakespeare is utilising both meanings of the word; Angelo has made a mistake, but he has also proved to be a hypocrite, pretending to be virtuous.

▲ A gold angel-noble showing the Archangel Michael defeating Satan in the form of a dragon

'figure': the primary meaning of 'figure' is character, but the Duke here introduces the extended image of coining by referring to the ducal stamp imposed on the metal. Angelo also uses the term on line 48, when he asks whether his character has been tested sufficiently to receive the ducal stamp.

Build critical skills

'False prints': explore how Shakespeare here continues the extended metaphor from minting coins.

▲ Balance scales, used for checking the weight of gold coins

Scales

Angelo plays on the image of coins being weighed to test whether they are counterfeit when he tells Isabella that his reputation will 'overweigh' her accusations (II.iv.158), and reiterates 'My false o'erweighs your true' (II.iv.171). Shakespeare links this image to the overall theme of the play, as he explores whether measure can be given for measure. Lucio accuses the Duke of being 'A very superficial, ignorant, unweighing fellow' (III.ii.121), which seems to suggest that the Duke's subjects think that he should have used the scales of justice more carefully to ensure that the punishment fits the crime. Indeed, the Duke accuses himself of being lacking in good judgement when he tells Friar Thomas that he has 'let slip' the statutes and laws he should have used to preserve order (I.iii.20–2).

Isabella, arrogantly thinking that Angelo and she are better than other people, tells Angelo that they cannot use the same standard to judge themselves and other men: 'We cannot weigh our brother with ourself' (II.ii.130). Shakespeare, however, has cleverly worded it so that she seems to be patronisingly saying that she does not expect such a high standard of morals from Claudio. This theme of how much people are worth is found elsewhere in the play, as, for instance, when Escalus declares that 'If any in Vienna be of worth' to be appointed the Duke's deputy, it is Angelo (I.i.22–4). The Provost comes to the conclusion that Abhorson and Pompey are as disreputable as each other; they 'weigh equally: a feather will turn the scale' (IV.ii.23).

When Angelo is trying to persuade Isabella to give him her body to save her brother's life, he argues that, if she were to do so, it 'Were equal poise of sin and charity' (II.iv.68). He judges that the sin of the act would weigh equally on balance scales with the charity of acting to save her brother's life.

The image of balance scales is used again when the Duke lists the things to be gained from the proposed bed trick; he argues that the corrupt deputy will be 'scaled' (III.i.239), or weighed in the scales of Justice. In the soliloquy in which the Duke debates the necessary qualities of a ruler, he argues that when a ruler judges others, he should be aware of his own faults and 'More, nor less to others paying/ Than by self-offences weighing' (III.ii.223–8).

In the final scene, when the Duke is pretending to disbelieve Isabella, he picks up this argument, saying that, if Angelo were guilty, 'He would have weighed thy brother by himself' (V.i.111). If Angelo had committed a similar crime, he would not have executed Claudio because he would then have deserved the same punishment. Ironically, Angelo said this himself, when he thought he was proof against temptation: **'When I that censure him do so offend,/ Let mine own judgement pattern out my death'** (II.i.29–30).

Top ten quotation

Language

'The importance of working on a text in this rigorous way – line by line, image by image, breath by breath – is that you discover what a speech is actually about instead of what you assumed it was about. In Shakespeare you must always play what's there, not what you think is there.'

(Juliet Stevenson, *Clamorous Voices*, 1988)

This is excellent advice for A-level students.

Verse

As one would expect in a play which moves from a brothel to a friary, from a prison to the court, the language varies enormously. Women were not allowed to act, so actors were ordinary men, regarded as not much better than vagrants on the social scale, and playwrights expected them to be convincing in a wide spectrum of roles. Shakespeare is brilliant at using language to help them to maintain the illusion that they are dukes or friars, nuns or prostitutes.

'I am a bit of a purist about the structure of Shakespeare's language. his metre – that basic ten-syllable iambic pentameter line – his rhythms, his pauses, his punctuation, where he breaks a line mid-way, you have to observe what he's doing with them, not as an end in itself but because they give you so many clues. There is a beat, there is a pulse in the verse that will tell you as much about the character as anything she says.'

(Juliet Stevenson, *Clamorous Voices*, 1988)

Plays were not intended to be naturalistic, and, to help these ordinary men sound like highly educated princes and judges, he let them speak in the elevated language of poetry. Even the servants respectfully speak in verse when addressing someone of high class. Poets harness the natural stress pattern of language, easily seen in the different forms of the word 'photograph'.

The basic noun has a stressed syllable followed by two unstressed ones: / ~ ~

photograph

If we add a 'y' on the end the pattern changes: ~ / ~ ~

photography

If we turn it into an adjective, the pattern changes again: ~ ~ / ~

photographic

Poets create patterns by using repetition. Each repeated pattern is called a **foot**, and there is a different name for each pattern. In his plays, however, Shakespeare tends to rely on one pattern of an unstressed syllable followed by a stressed one, (~/); this is called an **iambic foot**. Most of the time, his higher-class characters speak in **blank verse**, which is basically five iambic feet to a line and no rhyme at the end, for example:

~ / ~ / ~ / ~ / ~ /

Of government the properties to unfold

(NB Shakespeare would expect the actor to slur 'prop'ties' so that it is just two syllables.)

Regular blank verse moves at a steady walking pace, mirroring a heartbeat, but it is a very versatile medium. It can sound formal and carefully prepared, or spontaneous and colloquial. One easy device to pick out in an examination is a reversed iambic foot at the beginning of a line, when the character wishes to make a point by starting with a stressed syllable, for example:

/ ~ ~ / ~ / ~ / ~ /

Lent him our terror, dressed him with our love

Shakespeare varies the speed with judicious choice of words and with the introduction of pauses by employing short lines, although this can be interpreted in different ways.

For instance, when Isabella eventually understands what Angelo has been driving at, she ends on a short line of six syllables. Instead of having Angelo complete her line, which would suggest he speaks quickly, Shakespeare gives him another six-syllable line, suggesting a pause beforehand. She is taken aback and pauses before answering:

Isabella:	… ere I'd yield
	My body up to shame.
Angelo:	Then must your brother die.
Isabella:	And 'twere the cheaper way:

(II.iv.103–106)

Sometimes, the characters share a line which strongly suggests that Shakespeare wants them to dovetail their speeches quickly, possibly to suggest a mutual attraction. Here is an example of this:

Isabella:	Must he needs die?
Angelo:	Maiden, no remedy.
Isabella:	Yes: I do think that you might pardon him,
	And neither heaven nor man grieve at the mercy.
Angelo:	I will not do't.
Isabella:	But can you if you would?

(II.ii.49–52)

Taking it further ▶▶

Having rehearsed and performed the scene between Claudio and Isabella, consider:

- how Shakespeare's use of language (in particular, verse form) creates meaning and offers different ways to play the scene
- in what ways does the scene develop the characters and our understanding of their relationship, both past and present?

Because the movement of the verse is so simple and easy, Shakespeare can introduce any number of variations to suggest the state of mind of the speaker or speakers. When Shakespeare wants his actor to sound upset, he breaks up the lines with **cæsurae**, adds extra syllables or distorts the rhythm:

Isabella:	Tomorrow? Oh, that's sudden! Spare him, spare him! (~/~/~/~/~/~)

(II.ii.85)

Angelo:	What's this? What's this? Is this her fault or mine? (/~/~ ~~/~~/)

(II.ii.167)

cæsurae: internal breaks in the line, usually indicated by a mark of punctuation.

In this first interview between Isabella and Angelo, Lucio makes several short interruptions, but they are asides, outside the poetic form, as the two protagonists do not even hear him. It is interesting that, when Isabella promises to bribe Angelo next day, he also speaks outside the blank verse form, suggesting that he is completely taken by surprise: 'How? Bribe me?' (II.iv.151).

When Isabella is angry, Shakespeare reverses the iambic foot at the beginning of the line to help the actor spit out her contempt:

… but man, proud man,

Dressed in a little brief authority,	(/~~/~/~/~~)
Most ignorant of what he's most assured …	(//~~~/~/~/)

(II.ii.121–3)

Shakespeare also gives her **alliteration**, employing sharp plosives 'every pelting, petty officer' (II.ii.116) to convey her scorn. Poetry is not the natural mode of speech, but in Shakespeare's hands it sounds very convincing, and helps an actor create the illusion that she is a passionate young girl, only dimly aware of her power over men.

alliteration: a figure of speech in which consonant sounds are repeated to achieve a particular effect.

At times, Shakespeare employs a more rigid structure for his verse. The Duke speaks in rhyming couplets for his soliloquies after Lucio has been slandering him (III.ii.158–61) and while the Provost reads Angelo's message (IV.ii.94–9). In his soliloquy at the end of Act III, Shakespeare gives him rhyming couplets of shorter lines with only eight syllables. This unusual rhythm makes this speech stand out from the rest of the play, as if he is a Chorus, commenting on events and reminding the audience what they could be discussing during the interval.

Sometimes rhyming couplets are used to bring a scene neatly to a close; at other times they are used to suggest proverbial wisdom. Escalus is given two couplets in Act II, Scene i, lines 37–40, but their form does not mean that Shakespeare necessarily agrees that he should give up his defence of Claudio so easily. However, he has another at the end of the scene in which Shakespeare explains why he did not defend Claudio more vigorously: Claudio's execution is intended as a deterrent and, if they are merciful to him, the lawlessness will continue. Even Pompey has a rhyming couplet as he leaves the stage (II.i.218–19), reinforcing the argument that laws do not change human behaviour.

Close analysis of the ways in which Shakespeare tinkers with the basic pattern helps to suggest characters' thoughts and feelings. In the exam, you will gain no credit for saying that a speech is in blank verse, but it will impress the examiners if you point out variations and make intelligent speculations about why Shakespeare has varied the verse form.

Prose

Prose is the form of written language that is not organised according to formal patterns. It may have rhythm and devices such as repetition and balance, but they are not governed by a regularly sustained formal arrangement. Shakespeare usually uses prose for characters of lower social status and for informal and business discussions. So even gentlemen speak prose in the brothel, apart from Claudio, who, Mistress Overdone has already declared, is worth five thousand of her customers. The Provost, whose job has him talking to gentlemen, friars and prisoners, adapts his use of poetry and prose accordingly. In Act III, Scene i, Claudio and Isabella speak in blank verse which helps to heighten their emotions, until the arrival of the so-called friar, and then they both speak prose with him to suggest unprepared speech as the Duke responds to an unexpected occurrence.

It seems that prose is part of the Duke's disguise. In Act III, Scene ii, the so-called friar speaks prose with Elbow and then suddenly reverts to verse when he realises Pompey's occupation. By giving him poetry for this angry speech, Shakespeare signifies that he has forgotten his disguise and speaks as the Duke, interrupting Pompey, refusing to listen to his defence and ordering the Provost to take him to prison. He has a proverbial rhyming couplet and then Lucio enters and the Duke reverts to prose until Lucio leaves and Shakespeare gives him soliloquies in rhyming couplets.

Lucio disrupts order when he is on stage. Not only does he have prose interjections which are ignored in Act II, Scene ii, but he also disrupts the Duke's carefully stage-managed final scene. At first, Lucio conforms and speaks in verse, but, when Mariana enters, his unwelcome interruptions are in prose and Shakespeare lets the Duke show his annoyance by responding to him likewise, before returning to his carefully prepared script.

Balance

In a play whose central theme concerns achieving an appropriate balance, it is not surprising that Shakespeare has chosen to make some of his statements memorable by balancing them. He presents a thesis and then immediately offers the antithesis which is in opposition to the first statement, so:

Escalus: Some rise by sin and some by virtue fall.

(II.i.38)

The nouns 'sin' and 'virtue' are in opposition, as are the verbs 'rise' and 'fall'; the conjunction 'and' acts as the pivot. The statement is balanced, rather like a see-saw.

Isabella: To have what we would have, we speak not what we mean.

(II.iv.119)

This statement is given extra emphasis by being an **alexandrine**, and the comma acts as the pivot.

Other balanced statements rely on an inversion of the word order to create the counterbalancing effect (chiasmus), for example:

Duke: The goodness that is cheap in beauty makes beauty brief in goodness.

(III.i.177–8)

The Duke is given another example at the end of the play when he proposes marriage to Isabella:

What's mine is yours, and what is yours is mine.

(V.i.529)

It is interesting to note that Shakespeare elides the first two words in order to maintain the rhythm of the iambic pentameter.

alexandrine: a verse line of 12 syllables.

Vocabulary

Inevitably, there have been some changes in language since 400 years ago. Some words, for example 'lieger' (ambassador) (III.i.58) and 'bane' (poison) (I.ii.111), have fallen out of use, and others have changed meaning, for example 'punk' (prostitute) (V.i.178) and 'peculiar' (private) (I.ii.75).

Homophones and homographs

Sometimes the humour depends on puns on two meanings of a word which, although spelt differently, sounds the same (homophone), for example 'dolours', meaning diseases and sounding like dollars (I.ii.39). Sometimes puns are unintentional, depending on different meanings for the same word (homograph), as when Isabella tells Angelo 'I come to know your pleasure' and 'Heaven keep

TASK

As you re-read the play, check the notes in your edition carefully to make sure you know when words have changed meaning.

your honour' (II.iv.31–4). Previously, she was given a speech which plays on the sexual meaning of stones (II.ii.154–6), and Shakespeare reinforces this hidden meaning when she declares that she will not bribe Angelo with gold coins which have been tested for purity: 'Not with fond sickles of the tested gold' (II.ii.154). A neat homograph was used in the 2004 performance at the Globe, when Escalus referred to Angelo as 'Just ice' (III.ii.217).

Character differentiation

The characters have a distinctive way of speaking which helps the actor to create his or her personality.

Isabella

▲ Kate Nelligan as Isabella in a costume that emphasises her religious calling

Isabella is a novice, about to take holy orders, so Shakespeare gives her a semantic field of Christianity: *grace, mercy, soul, profanation, heaven, hell, damned, prayers, fasting, charity, chastity, sin, redemption.*

Angelo

Angelo is a Puritan (see **Contexts**, p. 66), and he is also given a semantic field of religion: *grace, heavens, tempted, pilgrimage, evil, saint, temptation, pray, sanctuary, charity, sin,* and, at the end, *my penitent heart.* He also uses words associated with the law: *jury, justice, judgement, condemn, fault, fine, recorded law, testimony, arrest.*

However, the most distinctive feature of his speech is his absolutism. He frequently uses the modal auxiliary verb 'must', which allows no possibility of deviation; he uses superlatives, for example 'most just law' and other words and phrases which reveal that he lacks compassion: 'Hoping you'll find good cause to whip them all' (II.i.121) and 'Dispose of her (Juliet)' (II.ii.17).

Elbow

Elbow's speech is distinctive because Shakespeare has given him a lot of malapropisms. Most of the humour in the scenes involving Elbow stems from his ambition to use sophisticated vocabulary; unfortunately for him, he usually uses a word that sounds vaguely similar but means something completely different, for example 'benefactors' for malefactors, 'cardinally' for carnally, 'honourable' for dishonourable. Elbow does make a pun on his name ('I do lean upon justice', II.i.46), but, given that he is portrayed as not understanding word meanings, it may be unintentional on his part.

> **modal auxiliary verb**: an auxiliary verb used to express modality, i.e. degrees of possibility or probability.
>
> **superlative**: the most extreme form of an adjective.
>
> **malapropism**: a confused, comically inaccurate use of long, sophisticated words (from the French *mal á propos*, meaning inappropriate).

> **TASK**
> Which other characters do you think have a distinctive way of speaking? How appropriate is it to their personalities?

▲ An early-seventeenth-century woodcut of Escalus and Elbow, demonstrating Escalus' sense of humour and Elbow's malapropisms

Contexts

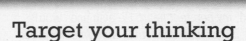

Target your thinking

- How does an awareness of Puritanism and the Virgin Martyrs of the Catholic Church help us to understand the characters of Angelo and Isabella? (**AO3**)
- How did Shakespeare adapt his sources to enable him to better explore his themes? (**AO4**)
- Can knowledge of actors' comments about the characters they have played help us to form our own opinions? (**AO5**)

Shakespeare's theatre

Taking it further ▶

If you have not been lucky enough to visit Shakespeare's Globe Theatre, watch the 2004 film of *Measure for Measure* or *Shakespeare in Love* to get an idea of the space Shakespeare was writing for.

In Shakespeare's day, theatres were modelled on inn courtyards in London in which the central area was surrounded by high buildings and there was only one entrance, large enough for a carriage to pass through. The first professional theatre was built in 1576.

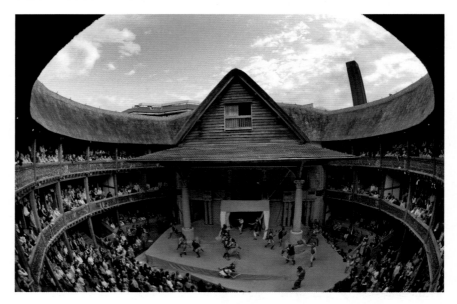

▲ The Globe Theatre in London

The theatre would have had a large stage, jutting out into the pit, where the poorer members of the audience would stand. There was a roof over the stage, and the galleries were roofed, but there was no other protection from the weather. The stage had two entrances at the back, either side of a curtained recess behind the stage. Above this curtained space was the minstrels' gallery where musicians would play and this could also be used as a balcony or castle wall. In this play, the director might put the Duke up there in Act III, Scene i, so the audience could see his reaction to the siblings' conversation, or he could stand in the recess behind the curtain.

There would have been a trap-door in the stage, from which Barnadine might have emerged in IV, iii, and a curtain round the stage to prevent the audience seeing underneath it. There were two thick pillars holding up the roof around which characters could hide temporarily or comic characters chase each other. To the roof were secured winches and other stage machinery designed to achieve special effects. Such a theatre could hold up to three thousand people and all the audience would be close to the stage because of the vertical sides.

Behind the stage was the tiring house, where the actors could keep and change their costumes, but there was very little room for storing props or scenery. When the scene changed from a brothel to a friary, or the court to the prison, there would be little indication except the often elaborate costumes of the characters on stage. Shakespeare's audience were used to using their imaginations. With no need to change scenery, the plays were fast-paced, the actors talking as they walk on, as in Act I, Scene iii, when the Duke and Friar Thomas enter in the middle of a conversation. Women were not allowed to act, so the young women like Juliet, Isabella and Mariana would have been played by boys, and the comic parts, such as Mistress Overdone, by actors like our pantomime dames.

The audience were drawn from most walks of life: the 'groundlings', standing in the pit, paid a penny; those sitting in the galleries paid twopence, and a seat in the 'lord's rooms' to the side of the stage would cost sixpence. A 'groundling' was a kind of fish, and they were probably given this nickname because they stared at the players in awe, with their mouths open. The louder members of the audience were the gallants, who went to see and be seen, and to show off how clever they were. Shakespeare's actors were always aware of the audience; indeed groundlings would be leaning on the stage itself. It was expected for the comic actors at least to interact with the spectators.

The playwright would read the script to the assembled company and a copy would be given to the Master of the Revels for licensing. The actors would not be given complete scripts, only their own speeches and their cues. After they had learned their parts, there would have been just one rehearsal before the first performance, because the company would perform a different play every day of the week, except Sunday. The actors would always perform in contemporary English dress, and the costumes were often very rich and elaborate. It would have created extra excitement to see ordinary men in the clothes of dukes and ladies, as the sumptuary laws ruled that people had to wear clothes that befitted their social station.

Taking it further ▶

If you are lucky enough to see a performance, either live or on film, of a play by Shakespeare in one of the theatres modelled on a Renaissance theatre, note how the company uses the facilities available and explore how you would use them in a production of *Measure for Measure*.

Aristocrats usually commissioned private performances at court or in a great house. Shakespeare's company, previously known as the Lord Chamberlain's Men, were adopted by King James on his accession to the throne, so they became the King's Men and performed at court more often than any of the rival companies.

Shakespeare's world

King James

James Stuart became King of England as well as Scotland on the death of Elizabeth I in 1603, and Shakespeare's company of players were honoured in being allowed to call themselves the King's Men. The first documented performance of *Measure for Measure* was in 1604, and it is possible that Shakespeare had known attributes of King James as he created the Duke. However, plays were subject to strict censorship, so Shakespeare conveniently moves the play to Vienna. King James admitted in his 1599 book *Basilikon Doron* ('The Gift of Kings') that he had been too lax at the beginning of his reign, just as the Duke admits ''twas my fault to give the people scope' (I.iii.36). This book was written for his son and contains general guidelines to follow to be an efficient monarch. The first part describes a king's duty towards God as a Christian, and the Duke believes 'He who the sword of heaven will bear/ Should be as holy as severe' (III.ii.223–4).

The second part of the book focuses on the roles and responsibilities in office. James encouraged his son to be a good king, as opposed to a 'tyrant', by establishing and executing laws as well as governing with justice and equality, balancing 'mortality and mercy' (I.i.44). He advocated the necessity of being well acquainted with his subjects and of studying the laws of his own kingdom and actively participating in the Council. The third part concerns proper behaviour in the daily lifestyle: 'Pattern in himself to know,/ Grace to stand, and virtue go' (III.ii.225–6). Also, in *Basilikon Doron*, James revealed that he was very sensitive to slander, 'the malice of the children of envy', just like the Duke who has two soliloquies complaining about 'back-wounding calumny' (III.ii.159), and is so wounded by Lucio's accusations that, when Lucio complains at his punishment, the Duke retorts 'Slandering a prince deserves it' (V.i.516).

CRITICAL VIEW

'The first years of James' reign were marked by a profounder questioning, but also by more explicit affirmations than Elizabethan times; and the need to hold on firmly to a middle way in the church, the state, and in private life was repeatedly stressed by the king himself.'

(J.W. Lever, Arden edition of *Measure for Measure*)

Position of women

Shakespeare gives a very clear portrayal of the position of a woman in early modern England. As the Duke tells Mariana in the final scene, if she is neither maid nor widow nor wife, she is nothing. Unless she was a widow, a woman, however high class, had no status and was not allowed to own property. Even high-class women were not allowed to participate in government, to go to school or university or to work. They would probably be tutored at home in those attributes which would make them attractive to a future husband; not academic subjects, but dancing, music, drawing, sewing and running a household. A woman's dowry was important as the future husband would have to provide everything for his wife, so it was legal to dissolve an engagement if the dowry was not forthcoming. She was not allowed to inherit money or a title and her closest male relative could dictate whom she married and withhold her dowry if he wanted to. If she married, everything she had, including her children, belonged to her husband.

The church supported the state's position, arguing that Eve had played the principal role in the fall of man. Saint Paul had a few words to say in the New Testament about the duty of women in marriage. 'Let the woman learn in silence with all subjection,' he advised, 'But I suffer not a woman to teach, nor to usurp authority over the man, but to be in silence.' Elsewhere he urged obedience: 'Wives, submit yourselves unto your own husbands.' Young wives who followed Paul's writings were 'discreet, chaste, keepers at home, good, obedient to their own husbands.'

King James enshrined the husband's authority in *Basilikon Doron*. In marriage, he told his son, 'Ye are the head, she is your body: it is your office to command, and hers to obey; but yet with such a sweet harmony, as she should be as ready to obey, as ye to command.' Shakespeare makes Isabella say what men want women to say when she admits to Angelo, 'Nay, call us ten times frail,/ For we are soft as our complexions are,/ And credulous to false prints.' However, she is making the point that women are easily taken in by a man's false persuasion. Angelo takes her words to be an admission that she is now prepared to give in to him and he tries more direct seduction, but this makes her uncomfortable and she strongly resists his advances.

Mariana did not fight Angelo's unfair slanders to her reputation but hid herself away from society. Isabella's reaction to her story is that she would be better off dead. Isabella's father is dead and her brother is presumably not wealthy as he has delayed his marriage to Juliet while her friends withhold her dowry. With no dowry, the only course open to Isabella is to become a nun, and this she embraces wholeheartedly.

Juliet is told by the so-called friar that her sin is 'heavier' than Claudio's, and the Provost tells the friar that she has 'blistered' her reputation. The use of the verb 'blister' refers to the fact that her womb is swollen, and reflects the fact that pregnancy in an unmarried woman was likened to a disease. It is also a reference to the fact that convicted prostitutes were branded on the forehead, so Juliet is now seen as an outcast. The Provost thinks that Claudio is 'more fit to do another such offence/ Than die for this', so he may lose his life, but his reputation is not 'blistered'. In Renaissance England, a woman must be pure, but it is not so important for a man.

Lucio, a gentleman, promised marriage to Kate Keepdown, but, when she fell pregnant, he reneged on this promise. Her reputation 'blistered', she presumably had no choice but to become a prostitute and let Mistress Overdone take care of the baby. If Claudio had been executed, what other course would have been open to Juliet, given that her 'friends' would not release her dowry for marriage with Claudio, and so would be unlikely to support her?

Puritanism

Predestination: the doctrine that all events have been willed by God. John Calvin interpreted predestination to mean that God willed eternal damnation for some people and salvation for others.

Puritanism was a religious reform movement that sought to 'purify' the Church of England of remnants of the Roman Catholic 'popery' after the Reformation. Puritans became noted for a spirit of moral and religious earnestness that informed their whole way of life, and they sought, through church reform, to make their lifestyle the pattern for the whole nation. This was combined with the doctrine of **predestination** inherited from Calvinism to produce a sense of themselves as the elect, chosen by God to live godly lives. This explains Angelo's belief that he is a 'saint' (II.ii.184), as well as the zeal with which he undertook his task of rooting out 'future evils' (II.ii.98). The name 'Puritan' was originally an insulting term, and, before they were known as 'Puritans' formally, they were called 'Precisionists'; Angelo is frequently referred to by the epithet 'precise' (I.iii.51).

Through the sixteenth century, the Puritan movement continued to grow. As they gained strength, Puritans were portrayed by their enemies as hair-splitters who slavishly followed their Bibles as guides to daily life; alternatively they were caricatured as licentious hypocrites who adopted a grave demeanour but exploited those whom they judged inadequate Christians. Shakespeare is tapping into a theatrical tradition of Puritans as secretly lecherous behind a façade of strict piety, but his Angelo is a much more complex character than previous stage villains.

Topical references

As well as allusions to the King's book, *Basilikon Doron*, the play contains a lot of other topical references. Isabella, for instance, refers to the contemporary belief that the spleen was the source of laughter (II.ii.126–7). Claudio's mention of 'the pendent world' (III.i.126) refers to contemporary images of the world hanging from heaven by a golden chain. Pompey's comment that 'Master Starvelackey the rapier and dagger man' (IV.iii.14) has been arrested reflects the fashion for a young gentleman to carry these weapons, as well as signifying a clampdown on fighting in the streets. Master Froth is a man of means because he has 'four score pound a year' (II.i.109–10); apparently, in 1603, James I required all Englishmen who had land worth forty pounds a year to accept a knighthood, or be fined.

Angelo compares the way his blood is suffocating his heart to the way 'obsequious' subjects crowd their ruler (II.iv.28); this may be a reference to the visit of King James to the Royal Exchange in March 1604. He intended to watch the merchants unobserved but he was recognised, and the crowds pressed round him so that the stair door had to be closed against them.

Just as comedians do now, Shakespeare's comic actors would raise laughs with contemporary references, many of which are not accessible to modern audiences, although actors frequently use hand gestures to try to explain them. In the brothel, much of the joking concerns sexually transmitted infections, which are no longer thought of as a laughing matter. In Shakespeare's day, there was no cure, but there were various useless treatments such as mercury, which makes people bald; hence the references in Act I, Scene ii to 'velvet' and 'piled'. Lucio says he will not drink after the first gentleman, because of the widespread fear that STIs could be caught by sharing a cup. 'Sciatica' was thought to be a symptom of syphilis, and the play on the word 'sound', meaning healthy, refers to the fact that syphilis affects the bones which would then 'sound' hollow. When Mistress Overdone laments that she has fewer customers because of the 'sweat', she could have been referring to either the sweating sickness brought to England by the soldiers of Henry VII, or another treatment for STIs in which patients were put in hot tubs to sweat it out. Pompey says later that 'she hath eaten up all her beef, and she herself is in the tub' (III.ii.50–1), referring both to the method of preserving beef by salting it in a tub and the treatment for STIs. Lucio's reply about a 'powdered bawd' is a reference to the powder tub, hence STIs, as well as face powder.

Some of the puns depend on contemporary knowledge of slang terms, such as Pompey's apparently innocent talk about 'stewed prunes', 'dishes', 'cracking the stones', etc. (II.i.). There is also sexual innuendo on the reference to a 'pick-lock' (III.ii.15), which was probably used to open a chastity belt; a chastity belt was an iron contraption into which a woman could be locked to prevent her having sexual intercourse with anyone but the key-holder. There is also sexual innuendo in Lucio's accusation that the Duke put a ducat in a beggar's 'clack-dish' (III. ii.111). Lucio's euphemism for sex, 'filling a bottle with a tundish' (III.ii.147) depends on the audience knowing that a tundish was a funnel used in brewing and so a phallic image. 'Untrussing' refers to untying the tags that were used to attach hose to doublets, and 'mutton' (III.i.154) was a slang term for a prostitute.

Punishments were very different in Shakespeare's day. Ordinary people were hanged by a hangman, who had the right to claim the clothes of the condemned person, so Abhorson says 'Every true man's apparel fits your thief' (IV.ii.34) when he is arguing, illogically, that tailors, the fitters of clothes, are skilled tradesmen, and so, as the hangman fits the clothes, he is also a skilled tradesman.

Gentlemen were executed, so Angelo demands Claudio's head as proof that he is dead. The Duke uses the torture instrument 'rack' (IV.i.61) as an image to describe how a man's reputation can be distorted by slanders. Lucio also makes a reference to the torture used to persuade people to talk when he says that marrying a prostitute is 'pressing to death' (V.i.514).

TASK

Watch the following clip:

www.youtube.com/watch?v=alMapfvRthc

The director, Robert Falls, and cast explore how to make *Measure for Measure* accessible to an American audience by setting it in New York in the 1970s. In what ways do you think the play lends itself to being updated?

Why Vienna?

England had been at war with Spain on and off since 1595. Peace negotiations were begun in autumn 1603 and culminated in a treaty signed by James in August 1604. The references to war and the possibility of peace actually refer to England's war with Spain. However, the censor would not allow any discussion of current foreign affairs on stage. Shakespeare, therefore, set his play in Vienna in order to evade censorship. Vienna was far enough away for Shakespeare not to risk a diplomatic incident with his negative portrayal of the city.

Another reason for the setting was that, at the beginning of the seventeenth century, Vienna was the capital city of the Holy Roman Empire. Since the Reformation, there had been no nunneries or friaries in England, so, as he wanted Isabella to be a novitiate nun, Shakespeare had to set the play in a Catholic country. Those saints, like Agatha, Agnes, Bibiana and Lucy, who had been tortured and killed in the protection of their virginity, taking their punishment with joy, would have been held up as role models, as they are to this day. The following quotation, taken from a Catholic website, demonstrates what Isabella has been taught:

The Virgin Martyrs as Models of Purity for Girls

Most of us will never have to resist to the point of shedding blood. But these holy martyrs have done just that. They have so much to teach us in every age. Their heroic virtues shine brightly over the bridge of time.

These Virgin Martyrs illuminate the darkness of a disordered culture that has forgotten the importance and the meaning of purity. May their zeal be a reminder that purity is a treasure to be guarded and protected at any cost.

(www.catholiccompany.com)

Marriage law

In Protestant England, nothing was required more than '*sponsalia per verba de praesenti*', a verbal contract to marry at the time the oath was taken, with the free consent of the parties expressed in any way sufficient to show their purpose. No banns, no public ceremony, no priest, no witnesses, and no specific form of words were necessary to make the marriage valid and indissoluble. However, the Roman Catholic Church had more stringent requirements.
The Council of Trent, held between 1545 and 1563 in Trento, Germany, and Bologna, northern Italy, was one of the Roman Catholic Church's most important ecumenical councils. Convened to counter the effects of Protestantism, in 1563 the Council passed a decree which stated that, whereas clandestine marriages had previously been declared valid, though blameworthy, all would be deemed invalid unless celebrated before a priest and at least two witnesses.

The Duke says that Angelo and Mariana had promised to marry each other and the date was set for the wedding. However, before the marriage could be solemnised, Mariana's brother and her dowry were lost in a shipwreck. Angelo treated the contract as a '*sponsalia per verba de futuro*', a verbal agreement to marry at some future time. Legally, such a contract could be dissolved by either party for good reason, and Angelo broke the contract because she failed to produce the dowry and because 'her reputation was disvalued/ In levity' (V.i.219–20).

The Duke refers to Angelo as 'her combinate husband', speaking of the couple as already joined together (III.i.211–12), and he claims that Angelo was 'pretending in her discoveries of dishonour' (III.i.215–16). The Duke and Mariana both treat the contract as '*sponsalia iurata*', a sworn contract to marry and a more binding exchange of oaths which could not be dissolved without the consent of both parties. Therefore, when Mariana pretends to be Isabella and sleeps with Angelo, she is keeping her oath and making Angelo keep his. The consummation of their union validates the contract according to the common law marriage, '*sponsalia per verba de praesenti*', and the religious ceremony conducted by Friar Peter at the end makes this contract valid according to the Roman Catholic Church.

Sources and influences

In the sixteenth and seventeenth centuries, audiences did not expect original plotlines. They expected to know what was going to happen and judged a playwright on how successfully he adapted existing stories.

The plot

Shakespeare derived his plot principally from two sources: a story in Giraldi Cinthio's 1565 *Hecatommithi* ('One Hundred Tales'), and a play by George Whetstone, *The Right Excellent and Famous Historye of Promos and Cassandra*, set in Hungary in 1578.

Cinthio's *Hecatommithi* is a collection of tales, like Chaucer's *Canterbury Tales*, framed within a sea voyage conducted by Roman fugitives. Occasionally, they rest and tell tales about human relationships. Each day has a theme, and the tale of Epitia illustrates ingratitude. The story of Epitia is a version of the story of the corrupt magistrate. In the primary version, a woman who pleads with a local authority on behalf of her husband, who is to be executed for murder, surrenders to the magistrate's desires in exchange for her husband's freedom. The wife keeps her side of the bargain, while her husband is put to death. She appeals for justice to the ruler of the land, who orders the magistrate to marry the woman and then executes the magistrate immediately after the wedding, thereby rehabilitating and revenging the wife. Cinthio makes significant innovations: Epitia is the sister, not the wife, of the condemned man, whose offence is not murder, but rape, and Epitia persuades the emperor not to execute the magistrate.

George Whetstone's *Promos and Cassandra* is a tragicomedy, based on this tale. Whetstone's dramatisation of the story of the self-righteous deputy, Promos, who seduces Cassandra by a promise of pardon to her condemned brother, is dramatised in two parts, each, after the orthodox classical pattern, divided into five acts. The reason for this complex structure is that he adds a comic subplot, in which the high-class prostitute, Lamia, is the chief figure. This subplot is closely linked to the main theme, as it heightens the impression of general social demoralisation and also of hypocrisy in Hungarian officials.

However, what is important to the student of *Measure for Measure* is not what Shakespeare took from his sources, but the effects of the adaptations he made:

- He developed Isabella's part, making her a novitiate nun and thus strengthening her resistance to Angelo's proposal, as she would regard fornication as a mortal sin. Also, she would believe that, if Claudio had allowed her to save him by giving in to Angelo's demands, he would have been damned as well.

- Shakespeare invented Mariana and the pre-contract with Angelo. Mariana enables Isabella's honour to be saved, gives a credible reason for Isabella to plead for Angelo's life and avoids Cinthio's and Whetstone's improbable ending whereby the young virgin is married to the man who raped her. Mariana, and also Juliet, give Shakespeare the opportunity to explore the nature of love.

- Angelo is developed from a straightforward villain into a complex character who is highly religious and severely puritanical with the potential to be a tragic hero.

- The Duke's part is significantly developed. Shakespeare adds his disguise and the way he takes control, manipulating events to a harmonious outcome. The story raises deep philosophical questions about justice and morality, rather than being a superficial tale with simple blackmail at its heart.

Taking it further ▶

Read the story of Epitia from *Hecatommithi* which Shakespeare used for his plot, and discuss in what other ways Shakespeare has improved on the original:

https://firstyear.
barnard.edu/
shakespeare/measure/
cinthio

- ◥ Claudio is made into a much more sympathetic character because, instead of raping Juliet as in the sources, their relationship is consensual and they are as good as married. Because of this, Angelo's harshness appears most unreasonable. Also – Claudio survives!

- ◥ Shakespeare also introduces Lucio, who not only provides much of the humour, but is used to undercut the Duke, the figure of authority, by exposing his paranoia about slander, and interrupting the Duke's carefully orchestrated dénouement.

The Gospels

The Authorised Version of the Bible was not published until 1611, a few years after the first performance of *Measure for Measure*. However, Shakespeare would have used other versions which are very similar. Christ's teaching is clearly reflected in the themes of the play. The title is inspired by one of Christ's tenets that if we judge others we can expect a similar judgement for ourselves.

Judge not, that ye be not judged. For with what judgement ye judge, ye shall be judged; and with what measure ye mete, it shall be measured to you again.

And why beholdest thou the mote that is in thy brother's eye, but considerest not the beam that is in thine own eye?

Thou hypocrite, first cast out the beam out of thine own eye; and then shalt thou see clearly to cast out the mote out of thy brother's eye.

(Matthew, 7:1–5)

Angelo is the obvious target for this admonition, as he condemns Claudio to death for the same sin he himself has committed. Before Angelo learned that he too was vulnerable to the same temptation, Escalus followed Christ's teaching and asked him to search his own conscience to find 'Whether you had not sometime in your life/ Erred in this point which now you censure him' (II.i.14–15). Isabella is more assertive and commands him to:

> ... Go to your bosom,
>
> Knock there, and ask your heart what it doth know
>
> That's like my brother's fault. If it confess
>
> A natural guiltiness such as is his,
>
> Let it not sound a thought upon your tongue
>
> Against my brother's life.

(II.ii.140–5)

However, this speech is followed by an aside that tells the audience that, even as she spoke, he was guilty of the same unclean thoughts as Claudio and so

Taking it further

Read the story of *Promos and Cassandra* which Shakespeare used for his plot, and discuss in what other ways Shakespeare has improved on the original:

web.uvic.ca/~mbest1/ engl366c2005/mm3.html

not open to reason. He spends the night searching his heart, but, instead of being moved to be merciful, he comes to the conclusion that his reputation is too important to him and he realises that he will be a hypocrite, full of 'false seeming' (II.iv.15).

> *You have heard that it was said by them of old time, Thou shalt not commit adultery.*
>
> *But I say unto you, That whosoever looketh on a woman to lust after her hath committed adultery with her already in his heart.*
>
> (Matthew, 5:27–8 and 15:19–20)

Being a committed Christian and a strict Puritan, Angelo feels that he is already defiled for lusting after Isabella, so he might as well give his 'sensual race the rein':

> *For out of the heart proceed evil thoughts, murders, adulteries, fornication, thefts, false witness, blasphemies:*
>
> *These are the things which defile a man.*
>
> (Matthew, 15:19)

> *Be ye therefore merciful, as your father also is merciful.*
>
> *Judge not, and ye shall not be judged: condemn not, and ye shall not be condemned: forgive, and ye shall be forgiven.*
>
> *Give, and it shall be given unto you; good measure, pressed down, and shaken together, and running over, shall men give into your bosom. For with the same measure that ye mete withal it shall be measured to you again.*
>
> (Luke, 6:36–8)

Isabella seems to be referring to this passage when she tells Angelo to model himself on God, the supreme judge:

> … How would you be
>
> If he, which is the top of judgement, should
>
> But judge you as you are? Oh, think on that,
>
> And mercy then will breathe within you lips
>
> Like man new made.
>
> (II.ii.77–81)

> *And he said unto them, 'Is a candle brought to be put under a bushel, or under a bed? and not to be set on a candlestick?*
>
> *'For there is nothing hid, which shall not be manifested; neither was any thing kept secret, but that it should come abroad.'*
>
> (Mark, 4:21–4)

The Duke refers to Christ's teaching when he tells Angelo not to be too modest:

> Heaven doth with us as we with torches do,
>
> Not light them for themselves: for if our virtues
>
> Did not go forth of us, 'twere all alike
>
> As if we had them not.

(I.i.32)

However, although the Duke quotes the Gospels, he has not followed their teaching; he has hidden himself away from his subjects so that there are all sorts of rumours about his depravity, as Lucio tells the Duke when he is disguised as the friar. The audience also soon learns that the Duke is being hypocritical in this speech as he suspects Angelo of being a 'seemer' (I.iii.55). The Duke seems to be flattering Angelo so that Angelo's true 'character' (I.i.27) will be exposed and his 'history/ Fully unfold' (I.i.28–9). We later learn that one of the motives for his disguise is to find a way to make Angelo marry Mariana. As he says in a soliloquy: 'Craft against vice I must apply' (III.ii.239).

Il Principe ('The Prince'), Niccolò Machiavelli

Machiavelli's *The Prince* (1513) explores the ways in which strong rulers assert their authority. The book is a treatise on statecraft, which accepts that the aims of princes can justify the use of immoral means to achieve those ends. His book was largely based on Cesare Borgia, the Duke seen here in the following extract:

> *When the duke took over the Romagna, he found that it had been controlled by impotent masters … so that the whole province was full of robbers, feuds and lawlessness of every description. To establish peace and reduce the land to obedience, he decided good government was needed, and he named Messer Remirro de Orca, a cruel and vigorous man, to whom he gave absolute powers. In short order this man pacified and unified the whole district, winning thereby great renown.*
>
> *But then the duke decided such excessive authority was no longer necessary, and feared it might become odious; so he set up a civil court in the middle of the province, with an excellent judge and a representative from each city. And because he knew that the recent harshness had generated some hatred, in order to clear the minds of the people and gain them over to his cause completely, he determined to make plain that whatever cruelty had occurred had come, not from him, but from the brutal character of the minister.*
>
> *Taking a proper occasion, therefore, he had him placed on the public square of Cesena one morning, in two pieces, with a piece of wood beside him and a bloody knife. The ferocity of this scene left the people at once stunned and satisfied.*

Taking it further ▶

Cheek by Jowl set their production in Russia today. What alterations to the script do you think they would have had to make in order to do this?

www.youtube.com/
watch?v=59-k2y-IUsQ

Unlike Cesare Borgia, the duke in _Measure for Measure_ admits that he is responsible for the corrupt state of Vienna. However, he dismisses Friar Thomas' point that it is his responsibility to put things right. He fears that ''Twould be my tyranny to strike and gall them/ For what I bid them do' (I.iii.37–8). So, like Cesare Borgia, he has 'on Angelo imposed the office' (I.iii.41) and given him 'My absolute power and place here in Vienna' (I.iii.14). He then wishes to disassociate himself from Angelo's methods to 'make plain that whatever cruelty had occurred had come, not from him', but from his deputy. He therefore planned a very public humiliation for Angelo, 'at the consecrated fount/ A league below the city' (IV.iii.89–90) and arranged for trumpets and various dignitaries to be present. He then acts the merciful ruler, publicly pardoning all miscreants, even Barnadine.

Critical history

The subject matter and the paucity of sympathetic characters make _Measure for Measure_ an uncomfortable play to watch. After its first recorded performance in December 1604, there are no further records of performances until the Restoration in 1660, when the low-life scenes and the emphasis on sex were cut in order to make the play acceptable to a more decorous audience. Productions all took the need for a happy ending for granted and often added elements of romantic courtship on the Duke's part.

In the seventeenth century, John Dryden dismissed the play as 'grounded on impossibilities, or at least so meanly written, that the comedy neither caused your mirth, nor the serious part your concernment' (_Dramatic Poetry of the Last Age_). Samuel Johnson, writing in the mid eighteenth century thought that 'the plot is rather intricate than artful' and that 'Angelo's crimes were such as must sufficiently justify punishment … and I believe every reader feels some indignation when he finds him spared.' Early in the nineteenth century, Samuel Taylor Coleridge called it 'a hateful work'. There were few productions and none true to the text, so critics approached the play as a novel, to be read rather than watched. One problem they found is the lack of characters they could wholeheartedly admire; it was felt they ought to be able to approve of the Duke and Isabella, but their behaviour was such that it was not possible. The themes of sexual corruption and the hypocrisy of the ruling class were unacceptable to a Victorian audience and so the play remained inside the covers of the book, available to literary but not dramatic critics.

The term 'problem play' was coined in 1896 by F.S. Boas to identify 'Dramas so singular in theme and temper (that they) cannot be strictly called comedies or tragedies.' He said that 'throughout these plays, we move along dim untrodden paths, and at the close our feeling is neither of simple joy nor pain.'

W.W. Lawrence, in 1931, suggested that the problem with the play was that Shakespeare was fusing elements from the world of legend and folk tale with complex legal and psychological issues.

TASK

How far do you agree that _Measure for Measure_ fits this definition of a problem play? Write two or three paragraphs giving your considered views.

He decided that the answer to the problem of the Duke was that he was a *stage duke* and so he should not be expected to behave in a plausible way. By contrast, in 1930, G. Wilson Knight saw the Duke as the prophet of universal forgiveness and mercy. He is 'compared to the Supreme Power' and puts into practice the teachings of Jesus. By the middle of the twentieth century, theatre companies had discovered the wealth of possibilities contained in the text, and it is more illuminating for our purposes to explore different interpretations on stage than to study critics who have only read the play.

Peter Brook's 1950 production at Stratford was the first to explore different ways of interpreting the text. Kenneth Tynan, in his book, *He That Plays the King: A View of the Theatre*, wrote about the 'grisly parade of cripples and deformities which Pompey introduces in that leprous Viennese gaol' which added to the 'ghastly comedy'. J.C. Trewin, in his biography of Peter Brook, wrote that he asked Barbara Jefford, who was playing Isabella, to wait as long as she felt the audience could stand it before she knelt to plead for Angelo's life:

> On some nights it would extend to two minutes. 'The device,' Brook said, 'became a voodoo pole – a silence in which all the inevitable elements of the evening came together, a silence in which the abstract notion of mercy became concrete for that moment to those present'.

In the early 1960s, productions 'began, increasingly, to present the Duke as the semi-allegorical God-like figure that some reviewers had been looking for in the mid-1950s and that literary critics had been discussing since the 1930s' (Jane Williamson, 'The Duke and Isabella on the Modern Stage', 1975). In the programme notes to his 1966 production at the Bristol Old Vic, Tyrone Guthrie argues that: 'he (the Duke) is a figure of Almighty God; a stern and crafty father to Angelo, a stern but kind father to Claudio, an elder brother to the Provost … and to Isabella, first a loving father and, eventually the Heavenly Bridegroom to whom at the beginning of the play she was betrothed.' However, not surprisingly, many critics were unconvinced by his interpretation.

It was not until John Barton's RSC production in 1970 that the happy ending was challenged and Isabella left alone on stage at the end. This was a turning point for the play and, since then, productions have explored the many different interpretations offered by the text.

CRITICAL VIEW

> 'Why stage this fascinating play – whose so-called problems are challenges to theatrical exploration – if one has nothing burning to say about it?'
>
> (Frank Rich, *New York Times*, 1989)

Taking it further

Draw a table identifying the romantic elements and the realistic issues. Consider how successfully Shakespeare has blended the two.

Productions have been imaginative in their attempts to stress its relevance to the modern world. In the 1987 production at the RSC, for instance:

most of our whores were rent-boys, run by Pompey, working a gents' toilet that rose from the floor. This was our attempt to de-anaesthetise the clichéd presentation of prostitutes in Shakespeare's plays, and thus shock and awaken our audience anew to the meaning of the scene.

(Roger Allam in *Players of Shakespeare 2*, 1988)

In 1991, Trevor Nunn focused on the psychological drama inherent in the play and thus found contemporary relevance:

Think of the Guildford Four or the Birmingham Six. An eminent judge can argue that it doesn't matter if innocent individuals suffer as long as the idea of the law is upheld and kept pure. Well, the distinction between law and justice is on every page of Measure for Measure … Or think of the immediate scepticism that greets Isabella when she accuses Angelo in the last scene. You can't open a newspaper without it being asked whether the victim of a rape can be believed when she says she did nothing to encourage it. And then, of course, there's the whole issue of the permissive society. It is extraordinary that Shakespeare should actually use the word 'permissive' [I.iii.39] …You think, 'I do not believe that this play was written in 1604.'

(Interview with Trevor Nunn by Benedict Nightingale, 2010)

Assessment Objectives and skills

> **AO1** Articulate informed, personal and creative responses to literary texts, using associated concepts and terminology, and coherent, accurate written expression
> - ◣ quality of argument
> - ◣ organisation of ideas
> - ◣ use of appropriate concepts and terminology
> - ◣ technical accuracy

This AO rewards your essay writing skills. Decide what your conclusion is before you start to write your answer. You should write fluently and accurately, structuring your essay carefully, linking your paragraphs, guiding your reader clearly through your line of argument and using the sophisticated vocabulary, including critical terminology, which is appropriate to an A-level essay. Use frequent embedded quotations to give evidence of close detailed knowledge, and demonstrate familiarity with the whole text.

> **AO2** Analyse ways in which meanings are shaped in literary texts

It is expected that students pay close attention to the methods used by writers to achieve their effects and use detailed and accurate quotations to support their points. Students may focus on:
- ◣ relevant aspects of form and genre
- ◣ relevant aspects of narrative structure
- ◣ relevant aspects of language, tone, imagery, etc.

> **AO3** Demonstrate understanding of the significance and influence of the contexts in which literary texts are written and received

Whether your essay deals with a single text or compares two or more texts, in comparative essays, the examiner expects that students will address the central issue of the question, as well as show awareness and understanding of a range of relevant contexts, some of them to do with the production of the texts at the time of writing, some to do with how the texts have been received over time and some to do with how the texts can be interpreted by readers now.

> **AO4** Explore connections across literary texts

To explore connections with other texts, you should try to find specific points of comparison, rather than merely generalising. In an essay on an individual text, this AO is still rewarded, so you could compare the play with Shakespeare's sources and influences, the Bible or other plays by Shakespeare.

> **AO5** Explore literary texts informed by different interpretations

For this AO, you can refer to the opinions of actors and critics, but you should also be alert to aspects of the play which are open to interpretation.

Individual syllabus information

Measure for Measure is currently set by the following examination boards:

AQA Spec A	Paper 1: 'Love Through the Ages' (examined, open, clean text) All AOs are assessed on this text
OCR	Paper 1: Drama and Poetry pre-1900 (examined, closed text) Only AO1, AO2 and AO5 are assessed on this text
Eduqas	Paper 2: (examined, closed text) One essay on both *Measure For Measure* and David Hare's *Murmuring Judges* All AOs will be assessed on this paper
Edexcel	Paper 1: (examined, open, clean text) Comedy core text. AO4 is not examined on this paper

For **AQA Specification A**, *Measure for Measure* is set for the theme of **'Love Through the Ages'**. At **AS level**, the paper is one and a half hours; there are two questions, each marked out of 25. The question on this text is in two parts: a passage-based question with a linked essay on the whole play.

The **A-level** paper is three hours; there are three questions, each marked out of 25. The question on this text involves discussing a statement with close analysis of a set passage as well as in the light of the whole play.

For **OCR**, **AS Level**, one and a half hours is given for this paper and you must answer two questions. There is a choice of two essays on *Measure for Measure*, each marked out of 30.

For **A Level**, there are two and a half hours allowed for two questions on this paper. The Shakespeare question is in two parts, both marked out of 15; the first part requires close analysis of an extract from the play and assesses AO2 and AO1. The second part asks students to consider a proposition using their knowledge of the play as a whole and assesses AO1 and AO5.

For **Eduqas**, **A level**, two hours are given for this paper and you must answer two questions; each essay is marked out of 60. Component 2 encourages students to explore the changing traditions of drama over time. There is a choice of two essays comparing *Measure for Measure* with David Hare's *Murmuring Judges.*

For **Edexcel**, **A level**, *Measure for Measure* is set for the theme of **'Comedy'**. Two and a quarter hours are given for this paper, and you must answer two questions. The Shakespeare essay is marked out of 35 and the essay on your other drama text out of 25. The Board provides an anthology of critical essays to support your study, but this may not be taken into the exam. AO4 is not assessed on this paper.

Meeting the Assessment Objectives

AO1	Articulate informed, personal and creative responses to literary texts, using associated concepts and terminology, and coherent, accurate written expression

Practise writing timed essays by hand, so that your writing remains legible and you are accustomed to shaping your essay within the specified time. Take care not to go over time or the other answer will suffer. Don't start writing straight away, even if other candidates do. If you take a few minutes to plan your answer and reach a conclusion, your essay will be more coherent and your line of argument easier to follow. Aim to write between 700 and 850 words, depending on the time allowed. Examiners appreciate succinct, legible essays which guide the reader through to a carefully planned conclusion. Plan your conclusion before you start to write, and always write a concluding paragraph, even if you are running out of time.

AO2	Analyse ways in which meanings are shaped in literary texts

You need to demonstrate how Shakespeare uses prose and the blank verse **form**, as well as how he uses dramatic devices such as soliloquies, dramatic irony, disguise and costume to explore his themes.

For **structure**, you could, for example, show that the play changes direction in Act III, Scene i, when the Duke stops being merely an observer and starts manoeuvring to take back control. The subplot reworks the themes of the main plot and Shakespeare neatly juxtaposes scenes to achieve a particular effect. It is also significant that Shakespeare holds back certain important information, such as Angelo's rejection of Mariana when her dowry was lost.

For **language**, you should explore Shakespeare's use of symbolism and imagery, as well as different semantic fields and plays on the meanings and sounds of words.

To gain high marks for this AO, it is a good idea to practise writing in analytical sentences, comprising a brief quotation or close reference, a definition or description of the feature you intend to analyse, an explanation of how Shakespeare has used this feature, and an evaluation of why he chose to use it, but not necessarily in that order:

Quotation	Definition of technical term	Explanation	Evaluation
Lucio's reference to 'cheek-roses',	a metaphorical compound noun,	is an appropriately flirtatious way for this reprobate to address a nun.	However, it acts as an implied stage direction, suggesting that Isabella either blushes when he calls her a virgin or else that she is annoyed at his impudence.

AO3 Demonstrate understanding of the significance and influence of the contexts in which literary texts are written and received

It is not knowledge of the contexts that is rewarded here, so don't write a lot of contextual material. The examiners are looking for an awareness and an understanding of the influence of a range of contexts.

AO4 Explore connections across literary texts

Only Eduqas asks for a comparative essay; however, in AQA and OCR, useful marks can be gained by discussing why Shakespeare has altered some of the details in his source material. You might focus on:

▼ Shakespeare's use of Christ's teaching as described in the Gospels in his exploration of the theme of balancing justice and mercy

▼ the ways in which Shakespeare has altered Cinthio's *Hecatommithi* and Whetstone's *Promos and Cassandra* in order to create a more complex and believable plot

▼ the influence of Machiavelli's *The Prince* on his creation of the character of the Duke.

Valid points can also be made by making brief but detailed comparisons with other plays by Shakespeare which are concerned with government, such as *The Tempest*, or have potentially good characters with a fatal flaw, such as *Macbeth* or *Othello*.

AO5 Explore literary texts informed by different interpretations

To fulfil the demands of this Assessment Objective, you can refer to the opinions of critics and actors, and you will also be rewarded for exploring different interpretations that you can offer from your own experience of the play, for example:

▼ *Measure for Measure* is difficult to categorise as there are elements of both tragedy and comedy

▼ the Duke can be interpreted as 'a kind of Providence', a Machiavellian politician, a benign ruler achieving self-knowledge or even a well-meaning man who is out of his depth

▼ Angelo can be played as a ruthless hypocrite or a sympathetic tragic hero with a fatal flaw

▼ the actor who plays Isabella also has ample opportunity to inhabit the part and find her own interpretation of some of the more unpleasant things Isabella says.

Building skills 1: Structuring your writing

This Building skills section focuses upon organising your written responses to convey your ideas as clearly and effectively as possible. More often than not, if your knowledge and understanding of *Measure for Measure* is sound, a disappointing mark or grade will be down to one of two common mistakes: misreading the question or failing to organise your response economically and effectively. In an examination you'll be lucky if you can demonstrate 5 per cent of what you know about *Measure for Measure*; luckily, if it's the right 5 per cent, that's all you need to gain full marks.

Understanding your examination

It's important to prepare for the specific type of response your examination body sets with regard to *Measure for Measure*. You need to know if your paper is **Open Book** or **Closed Book**, as the format of your assessment has major implications for the way you organise your response and dictates the depth and detail required to achieve a top band mark.

Open Book

In an Open Book exam, such as those set by AQA and Edexcel, when you have a copy of *Measure for Measure* on the desk in front of you, there can be no possible excuse for failing to quote relevantly, accurately and frequently. To gain a high mark, you are expected to focus in detail on specific passages. Remember, too, that you must not refer to any supporting material such as the Introduction contained within the set edition of your text. If an examiner suspects that you have been lifting chunks of unacknowledged material from such a source, they will refer your paper to the examining body for possible plagiarism. You will gain no credit for quoting the explanatory notes at the back of your edition or at the foot of the page.

Closed Book

In a Closed Book exam, such as those set by OCR and Eduqas, because the examiners are well aware that you do not have your text in front of you, their expectations will be different. While you are still expected to support your argument with relevant quotations, close textual references are also encouraged and rewarded. Again, since you will have had to memorise quotations, slight inaccuracies will not be severely punished. Rather than a forensically detailed analysis of a specific section of *Measure for Measure*, the examiner will expect you to range more broadly across the play to structure your response.

Step 1: Planning and beginning: locate the debate

A very common type of exam question invites you to open up a debate about the text by using various trigger words and phrases such as 'consider the view that…', or 'discuss how far you agree with this view?' When analysing this type of question, remember that exam questions never offer a view that makes no sense at all, nor one so blindingly obvious that all anyone can do is agree with it; there will always be a genuine interpretation at stake. They will expect you to offer evidence in agreement as well as evidence to refute the statement, and then come to a balanced conclusion. This means that, logically your introduction needs to address the terms of this debate and sketch out the outlines of how you intend to move the argument forward to orientate the reader. Since it is obviously going to be helpful if you actually know this before you start writing, you really do need to plan before you begin to write.

Plan your answer by collecting together points for and against the given view. Aim to see a stated opinion as an interesting way of focusing upon a key facet of *Measure for Measure*, like the following students.

Student A

This is the opening of an answer to the following AQA A-level style examination question:

'There is no true heroine in *Measure for Measure*.'

In the light of this view, discuss how Shakespeare presents women characters in this extract (Act II, Scene iii, lines 10–42), and elsewhere in the play.

This is the only scene in which Shakespeare lets Juliet speak, but it is vital to the play. Juliet proves that Claudio's claim that their love-making was 'mutual entertainment' is true, as her love for him is so great that she regrets the baby she carries prevents her from joining him at the execution block next day. She cries out against love because it is causing her such injury. Even though she has such a small part, by modern standards she can be called a heroine because she has admirable courage and devotion both to Claudio and to God. She is honest with God's representative, 'gladly' accepting his teaching, but firmly insisting that she repents her sin but does not regret it; she takes 'the shame with joy.'

Contemporary society's attitude towards her love, however, is condemnatory. The kindly Provost uses a metaphor comparing pregnancy outside marriage with a disease when he tells the so-called friar that she has 'blistered' her reputation. This is an oblique reference to her swollen womb, but also recalls the fact that prostitutes were branded on the forehead, so he also seems to be saying that she is now no better than a prostitute. She does not dispute this, saying that she bears 'the shame most patiently'. Patient has the double meaning of uncomplaining as well as suffering, so she is heroically acknowledging that society will make her suffer, but her love for Claudio is so great that she has no regrets. The Provost admits the double standards of this society in his sympathy for Claudio, 'more fit to do another such offence/ Than die for this.' Juliet also agrees with the Duke, in disguise as the friar, when he tells her that her sin is 'of a heavier kind than his'. Shakespeare may have had in mind the *Basilikon Doron*, in which King James told his son to choose a wife in the same way he would choose a servant, a horse or a dog, so women were of no more account than an animal.

Examiner's commentary

This student:

▾ addresses the key words of the question ('how', 'presents', 'heroine') in the first paragraph, setting up a strong line of argument to explore through the essay and demonstrating a perceptive understanding of the text

▾ analyses relevant aspects of structure and language in an assured manner

▾ pinpoints important quotations and integrates them into the syntax of the essay, confidently making valid points about aspects of love

▾ comments meaningfully on AO2 by exploring the metaphorical language

▾ expresses a confident personal view about the definition of a heroine

▾ reveals a perceptive awareness of the contemporary attitude to men and women who have sex outside marriage.

If the rest of the essay reached this level of performance it is likely the student would be on course to achieve a notional grade A.

Student B

This is the opening of an answer to the following OCR A Level style examination question part b):

'The play ends happily with order and justice restored.'

Using your knowledge of the play as a whole, show how far you agree with this view of *Measure for Measure*.

Remember to support your answer with reference to different interpretations.

It could indeed be argued that the play ends happily in the tradition of Shakespearean comedy. Three or possibly four marriages have been arranged; the villain, Angelo, has been exposed and forced to repent; the loyal Provost is rewarded with 'a worthier place', and nobody has been killed. Shakespeare engineers a very public return for the Duke who is back in charge dispensing the terror which he had 'lent' Angelo temporarily, and the love with which he had 'dressed' him. The power over life and death, memorably summarised in Shakespeare's alliterative phrase 'mortality and mercy', once more live in his tongue and heart, instead of Angelo's. The Duke seems happy that order is restored, but Shakespeare raises doubts that justice has been served. Justice is an abstract concept, based on people's sense of fairness, whereas the law is written down and therefore easily defined. Shakespeare demonstrates that Angelo interprets justice as following the law, whereas Isabella asks for fair play.

Isabella demands justice against Angelo, passionately repeating the word four times. Angelo declares that Claudio had been 'cut off by course of justice', referring to Claudio's supposed execution, the punishment set down in Viennese law. Shakespeare makes Isabella finish his line, suggesting that she pounces quickly on this claim, echoing his words disbelievingly, apparently recognising that the law is not necessarily the same as justice. Angelo hypocritically begs 'the scope of justice' so that he can find out who is behind the two women's accusations, but he is not really asking for justice; he seeks the full scope of man-made law so that he can escape a just and fair punishment for his evil behaviour. If the Duke hopes that pretending to still believe in Angelo's integrity was going to shame Angelo into confessing, he is disappointed, so presumably Shakespeare intends to suggest that he is deliberately lulling Angelo into a false sense of security so that he will reveal his own guilt.

Step 2: Developing and linking: go with the flow

In the main body of your writing, you need to thread your developing argument through each paragraph consistently and logically, referring back to the terms established by the question itself, rephrasing and reframing as you go. Ensure your essay doesn't disintegrate into a series of disconnected building blocks by creating a neat and stable bridge between one paragraph and the next. Use discourse markers (linking words and phrases, like 'however', 'although' and 'moreover') to connect the individual paragraphs of your essay and signpost the connections between different sections of your overarching argument.

Having set out an idea, in the next paragraph you might need to then support it by providing a further example; if so, signal this to the reader with a phrase such as '**Another** potential heroine is Mariana.' To change direction and challenge an idea by acknowledging that it is open to interpretation, you could begin the next paragraph with something like '**On the other hand**, Shakespeare does not develop Juliet's part sufficiently …' Another typical link is when you want to show that the original idea doesn't give the full picture. Here you could modify your original point with something like '**Although** it is possible to see Juliet as the heroine of the love story, Isabella …'

Student C

This sample is taken from the middle of an answer to the following OCR A Level style examination question part b):

'Angelo's offences are too great; he should not have been pardoned.'

Using your knowledge of the play as a whole, show how far you agree with this view of *Measure for Measure*.

Remember to support your answer with reference to different interpretations.

Nevertheless, although his offences are grave, no one is executed and the virgin he slept with was his wife by a previous contract. Shakespeare seems to be exploring whether a person should be punished for 'thought-crime'. Angelo is young and ambitious but lacking in experience; he was reluctant to be given the responsibility which the Duke, as he tells Friar Thomas, 'imposed' on him. Having been ordered to take power and told that 'Mortality and mercy in Vienna' lie in his hands, he tries to do a good job, cleaning up the city ruthlessly like Archangel Michael slaying the Devil in the form of a dragon on the coin which bears his name, the 'angel-noble'. He refers to the testing of gold and the minting of coins when he tries to decline the position: 'Let there be some more test made of my metal/ Before so noble and so great a figure/ Be stamped upon it.' Shakespeare reveals that Angelo is aware that he is not ready for such responsibility and perhaps doubts whether he will be able to live up to the high standards he set himself.

However, although his youth and inexperience do not excuse his crimes, his self-disgust at the 'filthy vices', which he rails at even as he plans to blackmail Isabella into bed, and his 'pride' in his 'gravity' suggest that, once he has lost his reputation for righteousness, a pardon will be more of a punishment than death. Shakespeare gives him a soliloquy in which he laments the execution of Claudio. The modal auxiliaries give the actor the opportunity to show that the guilt he feels when he says 'He should have lived' takes hold of him and a few lines later he says 'Would yet he had lived'. Placing the modal at the beginning of the statement lays emphasis on his regret as he now wishes that Claudio had not died. As he says after he has been exposed: 'so deep sticks it in my penitent heart/ That I crave death more willingly than mercy.'

> ### Examiner's commentary
> This student:
> ❑ confidently addresses the key words of the question – 'play as a whole', 'how far you agree' – and concentrates on the ways in which Shakespeare uses aspects of language and form to create meaning
> ❑ uses well-chosen discourse markers ('nevertheless', 'however' and 'although'), to signpost the flow of ideas
> ❑ creates good cohesion between paragraphs by clearly connecting the stages of the argument
> ❑ integrates and develops quotations fluently
> ❑ perceptively explores different interpretations for AO5.
>
> **If the rest of the essay reached this level of performance, it is likely the student would be on course to achieve a notional grade A.**

Step 3: Concluding: seal the deal

In your conclusion, you need to capture and clarify your response to the given view and make a relatively swift and elegant exit. Keep your final paragraph short and sweet; now is not the time to introduce any new points. However, don't just reword everything you have already just said either. Neat potential closers include:

❑ looping the last paragraph back to your introduction to suggest that you have now said all there is to say on the subject

❑ reflecting on your key points in order to reach a balanced overview

❑ ending with a punchy quotation that leaves the reader thinking

❑ discussing the contextual implications of the topic you have debated

❑ reversing expectations to end on an interesting alternative view

❑ stating why you think the main issue, theme or character under discussion is so central to the novel

❑ mentioning how different audiences over time might have responded to the topic.

Student D

This sample is taken from the conclusion of an answer to the following AQA A-level style examination question:

'In *Measure for Measure*, Mariana is the only character who suffers the pangs of unrequited love.'

In the light of this view, discuss how Shakespeare presents unrequited love in Act IV, Scene i, lines 1–15 and elsewhere in the play.

Just as Mariana's love grows 'more violent and unruly' because it is not reciprocated, so Angelo gives his 'sensual race the rein' when Isabella rejects his advances. Just as Mariana is prepared to risk everything in the gamble to trap Angelo into marriage, so Angelo risks everything when he threatens Isabella that, if she does not give herself to him, Claudio 'must not only die the death/ But thy unkindness shall his death draw out/ To lingering sufferance.' Mariana is not the only character to suffer the pangs of unrequited love; in Angelo's soliloquies we learn that he also 'feels/ The wanton stings and motions of the sense', and, because Isabella does not return his feelings, his lust becomes 'more violent and unruly'.

Examiner's commentary:

This student:

- ◄ loops the essay back to the question and the opening paragraph
- ◄ succinctly sums up the line of argument, repeating supporting quotations which have presumably been analysed earlier
- ◄ however, this student fails to consider the key difference between love and sexual desire
- ◄ ignores the craft of the playwright, writing about fictional constructs as if they are real people.

If the rest of the essay reached this level of performance, it is likely the student would be on course to achieve a notional grade C.

Building skills 2: Analysing texts in detail

Having worked through the previous section on structuring your writing, this section contains a range of annotated extracts from students' responses which will enable you to assess the extent to which these students have successfully demonstrated their writing skills and mastery of the Assessment Objectives. Each extract comes with a commentary to help you identify what each student is doing well and/or what changes they would need to make to their writing to target a higher grade.

The main focus here is on the ways in which you can successfully include analysis of language, structure and form to gain high marks for Assessment Objective 2. Since question one on the OCR paper is a close detailed analysis of an unseen passage, AO2 is not examined in question two.

Student A

This sample comes from an answer to the following possible examination task from OCR part a):

Discuss the following passage from Act III, Scene i, lines 48–114, exploring Shakespeare's use of language and its dramatic effects.

Shakespeare has built up the tension around this first meeting between brother and sister. Claudio told Lucio of his 'great hope' in her persuasiveness, and she sent word to him of her 'certain success'. In her soliloquy she expressed confidence in his 'mind of honour'. However, as she enters, she says 'Why' and then she does not finish the line. In this way, Shakespeare suggests that she hesitates for nine syllables before continuing, suggesting uncertainty. Shakespeare presents her as being unable to tell Claudio outright that he will be executed the next day and that there is an alternative. When Claudio asks her 'What's the comfort?', she picks up his word 'comfort' and gives it a religious meaning, using circumlocution to skirt round the truth. As Shakespeare builds her discomfort, he raises suspense in the audience: they know of Angelo's bargain and wonder when Isabella will reveal it and how Claudio will respond.

Shakespeare continues to build a sense of discomfort through his control of the dramatic verse. Isabella's speeches end on half-lines as if she is leaving a space for Claudio to speak and reassure her, but his responses are questions as he tries to make sense of her evasiveness. Her balanced statements use the metaphorical language of religion: 'free your life,/ But fetter you till death', and he interprets them literally. She then redefines his words 'perpetual durance' with religious meaning.

As the scene progresses, the suspense increases with Claudio's increasing frustration as he tries to interpret her words, and grows annoyed that she couches the truth in metaphors, 'flowery language', as if he is weak and cowardly. This part of the scene could be played so as to suggest that Claudio is increasingly desperate to know the truth directly. Four times he cuts short his sister's speeches with abrupt questions, until he stops her with an imperative comprising five short clear monosyllables: 'Let me know the point.' Even this does not elicit directness from Isabella, but the actor playing her might show even more uncertainty at this point.

When she says 'Oh I do fear thee, Claudio ...' there has been a shift. While the audience might at first think that she is afraid for Claudio's fate the next day, she is actually talking about being fearful of him choosing to live at the expense of his 'perpetual honour'. While it is his honour that she speaks of, it could be that, underlying this, there is a sense of fear for herself and of going through with Angelo's proposal. Shakespeare signals a cooling in the relationship between the siblings subtly through his use of pronouns. While earlier in the scene the characters both used the 'you' pronoun (which was common between members of the upper classes), Isabella is now distancing her brother by using the pronoun 'thee'.

She tactlessly stresses the suffering in death, whether of a beetle or a giant, and Shakespeare gives Claudio a resentful response, reassuring her of his courage. However, he speaks of death as 'darkness'; he has no confidence in the existence of heaven. When at last she tells him of Angelo's proposition, she uses a rhetorical question, 'Dost thou think, Claudio ...!', inviting him to be outraged. She has prepared him well, and he reacts as she has hoped with an absolute denial. Isabella, however, tactlessly warns him to be ready for his death 'tomorrow'. Shakespeare suggests that this sudden announcement sets him thinking, and he argues that for her to have sexual intercourse with Angelo is 'no sin,/ Or of the deadly seven it is the least.' He argues further that Angelo would not propose this if it would destroy his own chance of salvation. This speech ends on a pleading: 'Oh Isabel!' as Shakespeare prepares the audience for his harrowing speech expressing his fear of death.

> **Examiner's commentary:**
> ▼ **AO1:** Confident and informed response. Perceptive use of associated concepts and terminology. Well integrated quotations used to support relevant points.
> ▼ **AO2:** Close detailed analysis of language, structure and form and the ways in which Shakespeare uses them to shape meaning.
>
> **If the rest of the essay reached this level of performance it is likely the student would be on course to achieve a notional grade A.**

Student B

This sample comes from an answer to the following possible examination task from AQA A-level:

'Typically, texts present women as essentially submissive in the face of male dominance.'

In the light of this view, discuss how Shakespeare presents the relationship between Angelo and Isabella in this extract (II.iv.88–155) and elsewhere in the play.

Shakespeare presents Angelo's growing impatience with Isabella's failure to understand him, but he continues to present a hypothetical case concerning 'such a person', and to use euphemisms such as 'the treasures of your body'. While one production might play this as being a cunning lawyerly tactic, another might allow the audience to perceive nervousness in Angelo. This hitherto saintly, ascetic man might be feeling a powerful attraction towards her that he had never before felt, so he is unable to speak of his desires directly. Isabella responds to his words with passion, and, either angered or unconsciously excited by this, she picks up his imagery, arguing that she would undergo torture and death before giving her body up to shame. In the seventeenth century, the threat of eternal damnation for extra-marital sex was a very real one, especially to a nun. However, Shakespeare lets her fantasise about being a virgin martyr like some of the saints, but he gives her a semantic field from sado-masochistic sex: 'keen whips', 'rubies' (of blood), 'strip', 'bed', 'longing' and 'yield', which inflames Angelo's lust further.

Isabella apologises when Angelo accuses her of treating Claudio's sin as trivial, and, in her explanation, Shakespeare gives her a longer line, an alexandrine, with an antithetical balanced statement: 'To have what we would have, we speak not what we mean.' The balance of the statement reflects the way in which she is trying to balance her 'hate' of the sin and 'love' of her brother, as she points out in the next two lines. However, in accepting his reproof, she is not being submissive as she continues to argue that her brother should only die if he has been the only one to give in to temptation.

In his next statement, Angelo puts the blame on the woman as well, shamelessly arguing that it is understandable for a woman to be sexually wanton. Isabella accepts that women are easily taken in by men and Angelo takes her words to indicate that she is ready to give in. He encourages her to accept her destiny and act like a woman. Shakespeare has given him a significant homophone: 'if you be more, you're none (nun)'. If she holds fast to her belief in chastity, she will be a nun, but never fulfil her destined role as a woman. She humbly entreats him to leave the subject of male/female relationships and return to the subjects of law and religion. Believing that she is now submissive, Angelo tells her he loves her, and he soon finds out that he was completely mistaken.

Examiner's commentary:

- ◤ **AO1:** Confident and informed response. Perceptive use of associated concepts and terminology. Well integrated quotations used to support relevant points.
- ◤ **AO2:** Close detailed analysis of language, structure and form and the ways in which Shakespeare uses them to shape meaning.
- ◤ **AO3:** Well-integrated use of contextual ideas about sex.
- ◤ **AO5:** Begins to offer some alternatives – for example, in the ways Angelo could be played.

If the rest of the essay reached this level of performance it is likely the student would be on course to achieve a notional grade A.

Student C

This sample comes from an answer to the following possible examination task from OCR, part a):

Discuss the following passage from Act III, Scene i, lines 5–41, exploring Shakespeare's use of language and its dramatic effects.

Presumably, the Duke has already decided not to allow Claudio to be executed, but, in his disguise as Friar Lodowick, he must keep up the pretence. He goes to Claudio ostensibly to prepare him for death, but his speech concentrates on a description of life. A real friar may preach the futility of life on earth, but he would also make promises of greater glories in life after death. He would concentrate on helping Claudio to repent so that he could go to heaven instead of taking away his hope and telling him to 'Be absolute for death'.

After the first two lines, the Duke seems to forget his disguise and speaks to Death rather than Claudio; this makes the speech sound introspective, like a soliloquy in which the Duke attempts to find the meaning of life. He finds six different reasons not to value life, and he concentrates on the transitory quality of earthly pleasures and the inevitability of death. He seems to be in the middle of a deep personal crisis, thinking of death as a welcome release from his problems. This suggests that the play may actually be about his voyage of self-discovery.

Examiner's commentary

▼ **AO1:** Interesting overview and awareness of the importance of this speech to the play as a whole. Confident use of associated concepts and terminology.

▼ **AO2:** Some awareness of structure and form, but limited analysis of the ways in which Shakespeare uses language to shape meaning.

If the rest of the essay reached this level of performance it is likely the student would be on course to achieve a notional grade C.

Extended commentaries

The following three commentaries give close detailed analysis of key points in the play. They are not intended to reflect examination essays.

Balancing power and responsibility: Angelo and Isabella (II.ii.58–147)

In this exchange, Shakespeare addresses the question of what makes a good ruler. Isabella has agreed that Angelo cannot condemn the fault but not the perpetrator, but she argues that a ruler should exercise mercy. She is angered by Angelo's illogical assertion that it is too late, and Shakespeare gives her five stressed syllables, separated by punctuation, at the beginning of the line: 'Too late? Why no; I that do speak a word/ May call it again.' She demands that Angelo 'believe' that mercy is the most valuable attribute of a ruler. Line 64 is only four syllables; it seems that Shakespeare gives her a pause as she waits for him to speak. Significantly he has no reply to this argument. She then asserts that, if the positions were reversed, Claudio would have been merciful. Angelo does not try to argue back but asks her to go.

However, Isabella is now roused and will not give up. She invites him to see the situation from her point of view, and he can only fall back on the assertion that Claudio is a forfeit of the law. Cleverly, she counters his argument with Christian doctrine: all have sinned and their souls were forfeit once. Her stance is supported by the fact that she is dressed as a nun of the order of St Clare's, wearing white to symbolise her piety and purity. She reminds Angelo that Christ took upon himself the sins of the world, and she asks him 'How would you be/ If he, which is the top of judgement, should/ But judge you as you are?' Measure for Measure – if Angelo hopes for mercy, then he should exercise it. His response to this retelling of the Sermon on the Mount is to weakly take refuge in the law.

At last she is speaking fluently; she finishes his line (74), and Shakespeare uses enjambement in her speeches to run the lines together. Angelo cannot counter this overwhelming argument, but he still refuses to back down. What woman in Isabella's situation would accept his patronising response 'Be you content, fair maid'? Not only is the word 'content' inflammatory, but he follows it by telling her that her brother must die the next day. Shakespeare gives Angelo an alexandrine, a 12-syllable line, to put extra weight on the final word 'tomorrow'.

Five pauses on the next line, repetitions, mid-line cæsurae, extra syllables on some of the lines of Isabella's speech all help the actor to demonstrate her shock at this pronouncement. She soon rallies, however, and argues that the sentence is unfair. Not only is Claudio 'not prepared for death', but also many have committed the crime. Angelo has recovered in the face of her confusion, and he explains his ambition not only to punish wrong-doing, but to end 'future evils'. It seems that she accepts his argument because she begs him to show pity.

enjambement: in poetry, syntax that runs over the end of a line; run-on lines with no mark of punctuation at the end of the line.

His response to this is that justice and mercy are not opposites; in condemning Claudio, he is showing mercy to future possible victims of male lust because men will be deterred.

This argument highlights the fact that judgements cannot be given out indiscriminately because Claudio and Juliet are as good as married, so there is no danger that his offence will be repeated on another victim. Shakespeare has chosen his miscreant carefully, because it would be much more difficult to counter this argument if the condemned man were Lucio. Nobody has told Isabella, however, that her brother had entered into a pre-contract with Juliet and is as good as married; if Shakespeare had let her know this, there would have been no debate about the responsibilities of a man in authority.

Once again, Angelo patronisingly tells Isabella to 'be content'. At this she launches an attack, accusing him of behaving like a tyrant. Her contemptuous sarcasm is shown in the alliteration of plosives in 'pelting, petty', and the simile comparing a man who abuses his authority to 'an angry ape', performing foolish tricks. Three stressed syllables in 'man, proud man', followed by the Duke's own word 'Dressed' (I.i.19) really allow this woman to cut Angelo down to size, reminding him that his authority is temporary. Shakespeare reverses the iambic foot at the start of lines 118–20, 121–22 and 125 (see **Verse**, p. 56), allowing the actor to speak powerfully her accusation that Angelo is assuming God-like power over life and death, but his 'fantastic tricks' would make the angels weep or laugh, if they were capable of human emotion. Shakespeare has balanced the superlative forms in 'most ignorant of what he's most assured' as she accuses Angelo of arrogantly ignoring the knowledge that he was made in God's image and has been lent God's power.

Through Isabella, Shakespeare succinctly sums up the need for balance in a ruler. Her contemptuous outburst leaves Angelo speechless. Lucio, the Provost and Isabella all speak before he tries to answer. Claudio was right (I.ii.165–7); Isabella is an accomplished debater, gaining confidence and eloquence as she embraces the theme. After Lucio's first interruption, there is no evidence that Isabella hears him. However, his interruptions act as implied stage directions to the two protagonists and give the audience the first inkling that she is having a strong effect on Angelo.

There is a turning point in the scene on line 137, when Angelo acknowledges that she has won the argument by defensively asking why she is pointing out the difference between men with power and those without. She answers that those in power, although they are as guilty as ordinary men, cover over their vices with a skin which disguises them. Someone with 'authority', should examine himself first, and only through self-knowledge will a ruler be justified in passing sentence on others. The implication is that all men feel sexual desire and so are potential sinners. She is making him look to his own faults, and, ironically, he is forced to admit in an aside that he is guilty of lust. He is attracted to Isabella and the only way he can cope with this unfamiliar emotion is to walk away.

Brother and sister (III.i.115–51)

Claudio seems to assume that he will be damned, and he imagines death in 'horrible' concrete images, whereas both the Duke, disguised as the friar, and Isabella speak in abstracts. Claudio voices everybody's fear of death as he laments: **'to die and go we know not where'** in a speech which gains our sympathy and probably hardens our hearts against his sister. Death may mean **'fiery floods'** or **'thick-ribbed ice'**, being 'imprisoned in the viewless winds' or being 'worse than worst'. Claudio's fear seems to be making him understandably hysterical when he concludes that, however dreadful life is, it is a 'paradise' by comparison to 'what we fear of death'. The audience can readily sympathise with Claudio, and this serves to harden attitudes to Isabella. When he begs her to let him live, she reacts violently. However, it is difficult to understand why she is so angry. Is it fear for her own immortal soul or disgust at the idea of sex that upsets her? Could it be that she fears she might enjoy sexual intercourse? Her reaction to his fear suggests that she is not suited to life as a nun. She abuses him cruelly, accusing him of 'a kind of incest', and doubting that he is their father's son.

> Top ten quotation

Shakespeare puts two stressed syllables together at the beginning of line 145, and starts the words with plosives that allow the actor to almost spit out Isabella's contempt in 'Die, perish.' In her disgust, she even declares that she will 'pray a thousand prayers for thy death,/ No word to save thee.' She refuses to listen to him, and the last words she speaks to him in the play are to accuse him of being no better than Pompey, willing to profit from his sister's shame, and to hope he dies soon because mercy would give him more opportunities to indulge in shameful acts.

Isabella (V.i.20–59)

Shakespeare makes Isabella's first speech in this scene sound rehearsed. Her reluctance to lie about being a maid is revealed because she sounds as if she has prepared her speech employing some persuasive rhetorical devices. She demands 'Justice' opening on a reversed iambic foot (see **Verse**, p. 56) followed by a pause to give the word emphasis; she then repeats the word four times at the end of the speech, presumably building up to a crescendo. Shakespeare suggests that the Duke provokes her by passing judgement to Angelo, and she responds more passionately demanding that the Duke hears her complaint 'here', right now. Disbelievingly she echoes Angelo's words on line 35, and picks up his accusation that she will speak strangely. Five times she throws the word 'strange' back at him, punctuating her list of his sins, and she uses parallel sentence structures to build up to her climax. This time she does speak the truth, as far as she knows it, so her speech is fluent and powerful, but her next speech is calmer.

Once again, the Duke provokes her to desperation by saying she is mad and commanding that she be taken away. She responds calmly to persuade him that she is perfectly sane, urging him not to dismiss her claim just because it seems unlikely. The wickedest caitiff on the Earth 'May seem as shy, as grave, as just, as absolute/ As Angelo'; she speaks in measured iambs but adds an extra foot for emphasis. Shakespeare's use of an alexandrine (a line of 12 syllables) here suggests that the actor should speak slowly and deliberately. She ends on an antithetical statement: 'If he be less, he's nothing, but he's more,' lamenting that she has exhausted her vocabulary of wickedness.

Before studying this section, you should identify your own 'top ten' quotations. Choose those phrases or sentences that seem to capture a key theme or aspect of the text most aptly and memorably, and clearly identify what it is about your choices that makes each one so significant. No two people studying *Measure for Measure* will select exactly the same set, and it will be well worth comparing and defending your choices with the other students in your class.

When you have done this, look carefully at the following list of quotations and consider each one's possible significance within the play. Discuss the ways in which each might be used in an essay response to support your exploration of various elements of *Measure for Measure*. Consider what these quotations tell us about Shakespeare's ideas, themes and methods, as well as how far they may contribute to various potential ways of interpreting the text.

For you must know, we have with special soul
Elected him our absence to supply,
Lent him our terror, dressed him with our love,
(The Duke to Escalus, I.i.17–19)

1

> Having just told Escalus that his knowledge about Vienna, its people, its established laws and customs 'exceeds' his own, he then drops the bombshell that it is Angelo who will be his deputy in his absence. He vaguely declares that he has made this decision 'with special soul', suggesting that he has a particular reason, which he does not divulge. On line 19, Shakespeare has reversed the iambic foot at the beginning of the line to emphasise these key words: '<u>Lent</u> him our terror, <u>dressed</u> him with our love' (/~~/~/~~~/). The power is only temporary. Love might refer to his love for his people. His subjects' love for him and/or the Duke's love for Angelo; whichever he means, he says that it is only on the outside, like clothes. In this play, Shakespeare uses clothing imagery to signify pretence. Right at the start of the play, Shakespeare drops hints that the Duke has an ulterior motive for his actions and that his trust in Angelo is limited.

And Liberty plucks Justice by the nose,
The baby beats the nurse, and quite athwart
Goes all decorum.
(The Duke to Friar Thomas, I.iii.30–2)

2

> This quotation illustrates the lack of 'balance' in the state, the perils of liberty without restraint, and the way the Duke has neglected his duties as ruler. By personifying abstract concepts, Shakespeare is

able to draw on his audience's familiarity with morality plays. The Duke conjures up a vivid image of anarchy, in which the character representing Justice is being mocked and abused by the character who represents Liberty. This is followed by another vivid image of the overturning of natural order or 'decorum'.

3

Hence shall we see,
If power change purpose, what our seemers be.
(The Duke to Friar Thomas, I.iii.54–5)

> This is the first time the Duke admits that he has appointed Angelo not only so that he can restore order to the state, but also so that he can watch the deputy incognito and see whether power will present opportunities to reveal that Angelo is a hypocrite. In the light of this speech, we realise that the Duke was being deliberately ambiguous when he told Angelo: 'There is a kind of character in thy life/ That to th'observer doth thy history/ Fully unfold' (I.i.27–8). Ironically, the Duke himself is about abuse his power and become a 'seemer', adopt the disguise of a holy man, acting, as he tells Isabella, out of 'the love I have in doing good' (III.i.191).

4

When I that censure him do so offend,
Let mine own judgement pattern out my death
And nothing come in partial.
(Angelo to Escalus, II.i.29–31)

> Angelo's rectitude is absolute, and he declares that, if he were to offend as Claudio has done, he would expect no special treatment, but thinks his judgement now should act as a precedent for his own execution. Shakespeare foreshadows the later scene, but Angelo is sincere at this time, unaware that he is condemning himself to death. To his credit, when his guilt is finally exposed, he does not ask for mercy but craves death.

5

No ceremony that to great ones 'longs,
Not the king's crown, nor the deputed sword,
The marshal's truncheon, nor the judge's robe
Become them with one half so good a grace
As mercy does.
(Isabella to Angelo, II.ii.60–4:)

> In an echo of Portia's famous speech in *The Merchant of Venice*, Isabella teaches Angelo that, although powerful men have concrete symbols of their authority, mercy is 'above this sceptred sway'. Shakespeare has given her a pause at this point, as if she is waiting

for Angelo to finish the line, but he doesn't, and this suggests that he accepts the validity of her argument but is unwilling to back down.

Oh, injurious love
That respites me a life whose very comfort
Is still a dying horror!
(Juliet to the Provost, II.iii.40–2)

6

⟍ The love between Claudio and Juliet is mutual and so strong that Juliet cries out against love which is inflicting an injury on her; according to the law, she will be saved from execution because she is carrying a child, the fruit of their love. Paradoxically, what should be a 'comfort', her reprieve, is in fact is 'a dying horror', because of the thought of life without Claudio.

Ay, but to die and go we know not where,
To lie in cold obstruction and to rot,
This sensible warm motion to become
A kneaded clod, and the delighted spirit
To bathe in fiery floods or to reside
In thrilling region of thick-ribbed ice…
(Claudio to Isabella, III.i.118–23)

7

⟍ Like Hamlet, deterred from ending his life by fear of the 'undiscovered country' he would meet after death, Claudio has a speech which uses concrete imagery to express his fear of the unknown. He imagines his warm body, which has feeling and can move, lying trapped in a cold grave as it solidifies into 'a kneaded clod'. This monosyllable with its two plosive consonants (/k/ and /d/) has a solid finality which neatly contrasts with the 'delighted spirit' in the second half of the line. At the moment, his spirit is capable of feeling delight, and light illuminates it, in contrast to the 'fiery floods' of hell or the 'ice' of the cold purgatory which was thought to be the more fitting punishment for sins of passion. He seems to be responding to the so-called friar's homily, but whereas the Duke had tried to persuade him that there was nothing to regret in losing his life, he has failed to persuade him about the existence of life after death. This speech, with which we can genuinely empathise, hardens our response to Isabella and her romantic notion of martyrdom.

8
His unjust unkindness, that in all reason should have quenched her love, hath like an impediment in the current made it more violent and unruly.
(The Duke, in disguise, to Isabella, III.i.227–9)

> ⊣ Just as an impediment in a river makes the current more violent as the water struggles to get round the blockage, even so is Mariana's love more powerful because Angelo's unjustified accusations have prevented their relationship running smoothly. Shakespeare uses the abstract noun 'unkindness' in its modern meaning of cruelty as well as its archaic meaning of unnatural behaviour. This assertion that unrequited love grows stronger and more violent is also borne out by Angelo's behaviour; his love for Isabella is also unrequited and this makes him violent and cruel in his attempt to woo her.

9
A creature unprepared, unmeet for death,
And to transport him, in the mind he is,
Were damnable.
(The disguised Duke to the Provost, IV.iii.58–60)

> ⊣ In the previous scene, the so-called friar needed a head to send to Angelo, so he glibly declared 'Call your executioner, and off with Barnadine's head'. Now that the Duke has met the convict, he has learned that summary execution is 'damnable': it will damn the condemned man as well as the one who sends him to his death unprepared. He speaks of death as transporting the man to another place, as a journey, unlike Claudio who feared that death was an ending (III.i.118–28). Nevertheless, he still dismisses Barnadine as 'a creature', denying his essential humanity.

10
They say best men are moulded out of faults,
And for the most become much more the better
For being a little bad: so may my husband.
(Mariana to the Duke, V.i.432–4)

> ⊣ Mariana's love for Angelo is so strong that she refuses the Duke's offer of Angelo's possessions 'to buy you a better husband'. This is the point in the play which offers most hope for the future as Mariana is convinced that her love will restore Angelo and make him a better man. She could be right as, a short time later, he apologises and repents.

Website

**www.shakespearesglobe.com/discovery-space/adopt-an-actor/
archive/vincentio-played-by-mark-rylance**

– Very interesting transcripts of podcasts by Mark Rylance, former artistic
director of the Globe, made while the 2004 production was in preparation.

Films

1979: BBC: *Directed by Desmond Davies, starring Kate Nelligan, Kenneth Colley,
Tim Pigott-Smith.*

**http://bbcshakespeare.blogspot.co.uk/2013/10/measure-for-measure-
series-1-episode-5.html**

1994: BBC: *Directed by David Thacker, starring Juliet Aubrey, Tom Wilkinson,
Corin Redgrave.*

**www.ioffer.com/i/measure-for-measure-tom-wilkinson-shakespeare-
dvd-544796096**

Available from: **www.ioffer.com/gb**

2004: The Globe Theatre: *Directed by John Dove, starring Sophie Thompson,
Mark Rylance, Liam Brennan.*

**www.shakespearesglobe.com/discovery-space/adopt-an-actor/
archive/angelo-played-by-liam-brennan**

Available from: **www.ioffer.com/gb**: Interesting interviews in the interval with
Juliet Stevenson, David Starkey and John Dove.

Audio recording

2003: Arkangel CD: Starring Roger Allam, Simon Russell Beale and Stella
Gonet. ISBN: 9781932219210.

– This is a very good recording and an excellent revision aid as you can listen to
a clear rendition of the play while you read the text.

Books

Texts

◥ *Bate, J. and Rasmussen, E. (ed.) (2010) The RSC Shakespeare: Measure for
Measure (Macmillan).*
   – An edition which gives valuable insights into the play in performance.

◥ Gibbons, B. (ed.) (1991) *Measure for Measure* (Cambridge University Press).
— A clear and thorough edition of the play with a full, detailed and illuminating introduction.

Criticism

◥ *Cook, J. (1983) Shakespeare's Players (Harrap).*
— Some deep insights from actors and critics into the roles of Angelo and the Duke.

◥ Cook, J. (1980) *Women in Shakespeare* (Harrap).
— Thoughtful reflections from two actresses on the role of Isabella.

◥ Cookson, L. and Loughrey, B. (ed.) (1991) *Longman's Critical Essays on Measure for Measure* (Longman Group).
— Interesting essays on particular aspects of the play.

◥ Jackson, R. and Smallwood, R. (ed.) (1988) *Players of Shakespeare 2* (Cambridge University Press).
— Contains an excellent essay on playing the Duke by the actor, Daniel Massey.

◥ Jackson, R. and Smallwood, R. (ed.) (1994) *Players of Shakespeare 3* (Cambridge University Press).
— Contains an excellent essay on playing the Duke by the actor, Roger Allam.

◥ Rutter, C. (1988) *Clamorous Voices: Shakespeare's Women Today* (The Women's Press).
— Two actresses discuss their experiences of playing Isabella. There is some very useful analysis of Shakespeare's language and of different ways of interpreting the character. Of particular interest is a close detailed analysis of Isabella's first interview with Angelo. Essential reading.

◥ Stead, C.K. (ed.) (1971) *A Casebook: Shakespeare's Measure for Measure* (Palgrave Macmillan).
— A selection of critical essays, particularly interesting for study into the critical history of the play.

Resource Pack

◥ Cheek by Jowl (2007) Measure for Measure Education Pack & Livestream Recording (Barbican Education).

— A 27 page education pack comprising essays, interviews and classroom or homework exercises. The pack is integrated with a professional recording of the production, hosted online at www.cheekbyjowl.com/education.php